STAIRWAY TO DECEPTION

THE DEFILEMENT OF LISTENING TO AN EVIL REPORT

DR. MICHAEL D. SEDLER

IN APPRECIATION TO...

My church family. Thank you for your encouragement and support through this process.

Noreen Bechard and Debi Seier. For faithfully, carefully and lovingly reading this manuscript over and over and over...You are both a precious treasure to the Body of Christ.

Linette, George, Dana. God bless you for all your efforts and support.

Anne, Toni, Alma. Thank you for doing "one more" favor for me.

Apostle Steve and Patty Allen. You are an awesome breakthrough combination. Thank you for speaking into the lives of my family. You have our respect, love and support...always.

The team: Jerry and Mary, John and Chris, Bob and Melanie, George and Pamela, Dallas and Jody, Jim and Lisa...I love you all.

My Dad and Mom. You taught me to persevere and never give up. You helped me believe I could do anything. Indeed, all things are possible. All my love.

My loving wife Joyce and our three sons, Jason, Aaron and Luke. Your constant faith and love is incredible. Words can't express my appreciation, love and honor for you. I am, among men, most richly blessed.

WHAT PEOPLE AROUND THE WORLD ARE SAYING ABOUT *STAIRWAY TO DECEPTION*

As a senior minister who trains and networks with many ministers, I will be making this book a top priority. So many people need to be made aware of the enemy's number one tool of destruction, defiling God's people with an evil report.

> Pastor Peter Nicholes
> Southern Lights Christian Centre, Karingal, Australia

...We laughed at the wit and down-to-earth frankness. We wept as the Holy Spirit brought deep conviction. We are now armed to defend ourselves in the battle. This is certainly a topic that applies greatly to our nation of Mexico.

> Pastor Juan and Anna Guillen
> Templo Emmanuel, Acuña Coah, Mexico

When I started reading this, I thought of some people who always give evil reports. But soon, I noticed I am the one who often gives out evil reports. God's people need to know the results of evil reports. We need a church that reflects the awesome attributes of God.

> Pastor Yasuhiko Aoki
> Good Samaritan Church, Inagawa City, Hyogo, Japan

Finally, a new book that will save lives! Dr. Michael Sedler has written a compelling, illuminating, and above all, convincing book detailing how offense opens the door to deception. As a part of my pastoral team, Dr. Sedler's work has brought new understanding and freedom into the life of our local church. There may be only a handful of books every year that combine sound biblical theology with practical application. This is one of those books and is a must read for all who mean business with God.

> Dr. Stephen G. Allen, Senior Pastor
> Harvest Christian Fellowship, Spokane, WA.

STAIRWAY TO DECEPTION BY MICHAEL SEDLER

Published by Christian Life Publications

Copyright © 1999 by Michael Sedler
This book or parts thereof may not be reproduced in any form without prior written permission from the author.

ISBN 0-9675153-0-0

Unless otherwise noted, all scripture quotations are from the New King James Version of the Bible. Copyright 1979, 1980, 1982, 1988 by Thomas Nelson, Inc., publishers. Used by permission.

Scripture quotations marked by KJV are from the King James Version of the Bible.

Scripture quotations marked CEV are from the Holy Bible, Contemporary English Version. Copyright 1995. American Bible Society. Used by permission

The names of certain persons mentioned in this book have been changed in order to protect the privacy of the individuals involved.

Cover Design: Dana Salsbury
Illustrations: George Anderson
Project Layout: Linette Schmaltz

TABLE OF CONTENTS

Chapter 1	Defining an Evil or False Report	1
Chapter 2	Recognizing Carriers of an Evil Report	13
Chapter 3	Initial Responses to an Evil Report	27
Chapter 4	Confusion	43
Chapter 5	Contamination	65
Chapter 6	Foolishness	83
Chapter 7	Identification	105
Chapter 8	Fear	123
Chapter 9	Impurity	145
Chapter 10	Deception	163
Chapter 11	The Cleansing Process	187
Chapter 12	Closer to Home	213

INTRODUCTION

In my years as a "born-again" Christian, I have heard many teachings and presentations on the evils of gossip, slander and murmuring. The majority of these teachings have focused on restraining ourselves from speaking negatively about other people. It is difficult to be successful in this arena. My desire, as is the case with most of my Christian brothers and sisters, has been to be pure before Christ, and to bridle my tongue. However, time and time again, I find myself speaking evil of others and being involved in ungodly conversations. This is not only confusing, also frustrating.

Many years ago, while traveling on vacation with my family, we stopped at a church in southeast Idaho. A visiting minister began to share about the impact of listening to evil reports. (I later found out this material was from Bill Gothard's seminar in "Basic Youth Conflicts.") The spirit of conviction fell upon me and I began a long process of synthesizing the information to fully understand its implications in my Christian walk. As God unfolded truth to me in this area, I realized I had been missing an important component of my struggle. Yes, it is true, fleshly thoughts and ideas are a problem; the tongue must be controlled; I should not speak evil or negatively of others. However, this constant battle was only a symptom of a much greater problem.

God began to reveal areas of my life that fell prey to the spirit of deception in the area of conversation. There were many times when I did not speak a word, yet my very presence "screamed" support for the conversation at hand. These "innocent" situations seemed to be more the rule than the exception. This was disconcerting as I truly had sought for Christ's character within my life. After many hours, days and months of seeking God for understanding, He slowly revealed specific reasons for my constant stumbling. In looking back over the years, I realize the slowness of God's presentation had nothing to do with Him and everything to do with my shortsightedness and my inability to grasp the magnitude of the problem.

It is the purpose of this book to clearly define and emphasize the magnitude of injury that takes place when we are involved in negative conversations. The Bible refers to negative comments or stories regarding other people as "evil reports." This may seem a strong term, but careful research of the scriptures shows that our "gossip" and "truth-stretching" are much more than idle chatter. This type of speech carries with it far-reaching ramifications that not only affect the life of the speaker but the life of the listener. It is a life and death issue. It is both "speaking evil" and **listening to evil reports** that defile each one of our spirits.

The Spirit of God desires to touch us, to show us areas where *we may have been defiled by evil reports.* I believe the Holy Spirit will help us break away from the enslavement of ungodly habits and allow us **to *not* give ear** to sinful speech patterns. *"An evildoer gives heed to false lips; A liar listens eagerly to a spiteful tongue"* (Prov. 17:4). We will become free from listening to evil reports and our own tongues will be restrained from speaking evil of others.

I encourage you to open your mind, heart and spirit to investigate the part you may play in perpetuating evil or false reports. Be prepared to be challenged, even provoked by this book. The topic is not comfortable nor are the repercussions of listening to an evil report. Let the Holy Spirit shine light upon each dark, hidden recess of your soul. My time of study, prayer and research has opened a door for me to receive revelation from God, and to be touched by His cleansing power. I pray that God's powerful and gentle hands will rest upon each reader to bring purification, illumination and revelation.

I wish to give special thanks and blessings to Mr. Bill Gothard for his inspiration in this area. His willingness to allow me to use some of his material enabled me to build a strong foundation for this book.

DEFINING AN EVIL REPORT

CHAPTER 1

DEFINING AN EVIL OR FALSE REPORT

The world tells us that it is okay to speak negatively about one another. The newspapers, television, magazines and media, in general, make millions of dollars by exploiting people and by "sharing" their misfortune. Our T.V. talk shows never tire of exposing people, or of creating a scandalous atmosphere. We are so ingrained and brainwashed into believing that it is permissible to verbally violate one another that it takes a concentrated effort to begin to have new thought patterns. Our words may create injury and pain in someone's life, yet we seem oblivious to the results. As the pages of this book unfold, take time to pray, discuss the topic with others and begin to allow God to *"transform you by the renewing of your mind"* (Rom. 12:2).

- Aren't gossip and false reports just a way of life? Is it really possible not to speak against people?
- How can one recognize an evil report?

- Is there ever a time to talk about someone and have it not be considered an evil report?
- Is it still an evil report if the person did not intend to create injury toward another person?
- How can I respond in a biblical way to people who gossip and murmur?

Each of these areas will be addressed, with an emphasis on how to recognize individuals who carry a spirit of negativism and gossip. Different stairsteps (or levels) of defilement and how they impact an individual's spiritual walk with God will be presented. Each stairstep will draw us closer to the arena of deception.

- What causes someone to listen to impure or ungodly conversation?
- How can we be cleansed from the violation that occurs when we listen to one of these reports?

These issues will be explained in this book, along with biblical responses to those who attempt to violate others with their speech. Positive and effective strategies that prevent us from becoming "evil reporters" will also be presented.

What Is an Evil or False Report?

We often think of the word *gossip* when talking about an evil report. This is only a small part of what the Bible refers to as "an evil or false report." Noah Webster's 1828 dictionary states that the word *evil* means, "having bad qualities of a moral kind; wicked; corrupt; perverse; producing sorrow, distress, injury or calamity." An evil report is not only what is said, but how it is said, our attitude, and even the condition of our heart. Let's give some substance to the term, "evil report." One working definition we will use is:

An individual, maliciously, using words or attitude, causes injury, damage or discredit to another's reputation or character.

Obviously, a false report creates damage to an individual. Words are often casually and carelessly used without any thought to the repercussions in another person's life. Comments such as, "Did you hear what Tom said?" or, "I am really offended at Sally, do you know what she did?" create hurt and separation from a brother or sister in Christ. Is this the way to build up the Body of Christ? Imagine how edifying and encouraging words of gossip are to Tom or Sally! I'm sure they would hardly be able to wait to be "blessed" like that again. This type of speech pattern would continue to degrade people, eventually creating an atmosphere that provoked others to move into serious sin. Perhaps a new ministry could be started—"The Ministry of Hurts;" or maybe one could become "The Prophet of Put-Downs." Some may laugh at such ludicrous statements, yet Father God is not laughing. He doesn't find our cold, callous statements about His children amusing. Now, don't get defensive so early in this book! You will have plenty of time later to get upset—or rather, convicted.

The severity and seriousness of God's conviction in my life regarding these exact areas is far from humorous. These areas are so serious that they might disqualify individuals from ministry opportunities. Proverbs 10:18b says, "...*And whoever spreads slander is a fool.*" I remember hearing someone say, "It is better to have your mouth closed and let people think you are foolish than to open your mouth and let them know you are foolish." We have all heard it said that "Actions speak louder than words," or, "One picture is worth a thousand words." In this case, our words speak volumes; they paint a vivid picture. Unfortunately, the magnitude of the words spoken paints the picture of hurt and injury in people's lives. God holds us accountable for the words we speak to one another. Our careless ways of speaking cannot be chalked up to "I didn't know better," or "I was only kidding." To be "Christ-like" is to walk a path of integrity, purity and commitment in all our relationships and interactions.

I know of two young people who have been discussing marriage. This is an exciting topic among their social circle. When asked about the possibility of getting engaged, the man responded, "slowly and surely, we'll be engaged." One of the people who had overheard part of the conversation turned toward a friend and said, "Who and Shirley are getting engaged? And who's Shirley?" It is so easy to take a comment, twist it and run with it. Our words are like toothpaste coming out of the tube. It flows out so easily, yet is impossible to put back into the container. To prevent further loss of toothpaste, we need to take the cap and place it over the tube. And with people, the cap (mouth) needs to be closed with haste, before words flow out too quickly.

Let me take another approach. Imagine filling out a "spiritual job application." How would you answer the following questions?

1. Do you speak evil of others?
2. When you are hurt by another person's insensitivity, do you lovingly confront them, or do you share the frustration with others?
3. If Christ was listening to each of your conversations (and He is), would the content be offensive to Him?
4. When you disagree with your supervisor, who else is going to know about it?

For those who are married, change the phrases a bit and try this test. Instead of "another person's" or "supervisor," put in the word *spouse*. **Ouch!** And young people, you can substitute the word *parent(s)*.

The Bible tells us that as believers in Christ, we are His Bride. It is imperative for the "Church," referring to all Christians, to seek God and ask Him to cut away at those areas of our lives that cause us to stumble. God is calling His Bride to be purified, to be cleansed and to be undefiled. We must prepare for the daily walk of faith which God has asked of His children; we must confront our character flaws; we must be accountable to one another; we must cleanse our speech and our life patterns; we must commit our lives to Christ, and seek unity amongst the brethren. I hope that the proverbial "light bulb" is beginning to come on in your mind. Revelation in this area will allow each of us to ward off the attacks of the enemy. We must cleanse our spirits so that we may hear the pure word of God without contamination.

Tested by Fire

The third chapter in the Book of Daniel relates the story of Daniel's three Hebrew companions. Their names were Hananiah, Mishael and Azariah. While these names may not be familiar, their Babylonian names are more recognizable—Shadrach, Meshach and Abednego. It was during the reign of King Nebuchadnezzar that a golden idol was erected. All the people in the province were to fall down and worship the golden image which King Nebuchadnezzar had ordered to be built. His command was that all who refused to fall down would be cast into a fiery furnace, thereby being consumed by the heat and flames. However, the three Hebrew men refused to bow down.

When people take a stand for God, a separation of those who desire more of God from those who desire more of the flesh begins. Because Shadrach, Meshach and Abednego refused to bow down to a false god, there arose a murmuring among some of the people who promptly went to the king and gave an evil report about them. The intent of the report was to "cause injury and damage" (actually death) to the three Hebrew men. The king's anger was great. He had the three men brought before him, confirmed their refusal to bow down to the idol, and had them thrown into a furnace of fire. The soldiers and king looked on, anticipating the young men's incineration. Before their eyes, a fourth figure appeared within the furnace.

> *Then King Nebuchadnezzar was astonished; and he rose in haste and spoke, saying to his counselors, "Did we not cast three men bound into the midst of the fire?" They answered and said to the king, "True, o king." "Look!" he answered, "I see four men loose, walking in the midst of the fire; and they are not hurt, and the form of the fourth is like the Son of God."*
>
> Dan. 3:24, 25

Astonished and somewhat in fear, the king released Shadrach, Meshach and Abednego, and immediately promoted them to a position of honor within the province.

This is an inspiring and exciting account about people of faith. It would seem that all participants were blessed and found favor in God's sight. But what of Nebuchadnezzar? Was he defiled and contaminated as one who "listened to an evil report?" Were there repercussions for him for listening to ungodly words and for not repenting to God? What can happen to those who come against God's anointed people, whether in words or deeds?

By listening to an evil report, the king became polluted. His perspective of the situation was skewed toward injuring the three men. Without seeking further information,

King Nebuchadnezzar chose to take the life of three people because of a negative report. In Daniel, chapter 4, we find the rest of the story regarding the king, the one who **did not** initiate an evil report against the Hebrew men, **but** *listened* and thereby, became defiled by the report. The king rose up in pride and arrogance. He spoke of *his* accomplishments and *his* achievements.

> *At the end of twelve months he (Nebuchadnezzar) was walking about the royal palace of Babylon. The king spoke, saying, "Is not this great Babylon, that **I** have built for a royal dwelling by **my** mighty power and for the honor of **my** majesty?" While the word was still in the king's mouth, a voice fell from heaven: "King Nebuchadnezzar, to you it is spoken: the kingdom has departed from you!"*
>
> Dan. 4:29-30 (emphasis added)

Defilement will often take the form of pride and selfishness. Due to his self-centered approach, King Nebuchadnezzar's kingdom was taken from him. He was humiliated and lived for a time in the fields, eating grass like an animal. However, in time, he repented, turned his heart back toward God and was restored.

> *"At the same time my reason returned to me, and for the glory of my kingdom, my honor and splendor returned to me. My counselors and nobles resorted to me, I was restored to my kingdom, and excellent majesty was added to me. Now I, Nebuchadnezzar, praise and extol and honor the King of heaven, all of whose works are truth, and His ways justice. And those who walk in pride He is able to put down."*
>
> Dan. 4:36-37

Just listening can create tremendous damage to your perspective, viewpoint and overall spirit. Nebuchadnezzar should not have allowed himself to be part of the plot to destroy the Hebrew people. His refusal to ask questions, gain clarification and remove himself from the plan of destruction led to an impurity in his own spirit.

This is a very serious issue in the kingdom of God. Our Lord does not want talebearers and false witnesses against other people. If we expect to be a light to the world, our lives must represent purity and godliness. A small conversation or a negative comment may destroy the testimony of a life. Listening to such grumbling and attitudes eventually contaminate the spirit. The more we allow discontentment to be taken in by our spirit, the greater the tendency to compromise our own speech patterns. We are being called to a high standard of living where the rewards for our faithfulness are eternal. I refuse to succumb to Satan's wily methods! The stakes are high, but thankfully, we are on the winning team.

QUESTIONS—Examining the Heart

1. In your own life, have you developed patterns in your speech that would be considered to be evil reports (as defined in this chapter)?

2. When you were growing up, were gossip, rumors, false reporting encouraged, modeled or demonstrated by the adults in the home?

3. Think back over the years and try to remember if the topic of this book has been taught in your church? Your home? Your school?

RECOGNIZING CARRIERS OF AN EVIL REPORT

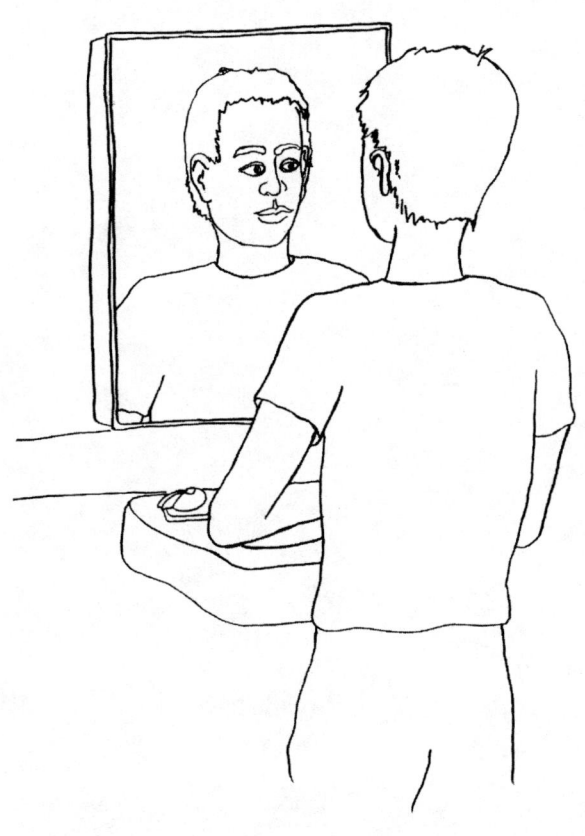

CHAPTER 2

RECOGNIZING CARRIERS OF AN EVIL REPORT

As a youth in Phoenix, Arizona, I played baseball during my elementary and high school years. I was the fortunate recipient of a scholarship and played baseball at a university in San Diego, California. I learned a great deal from my high school and college coaches about preparing to play against a team and about the pitcher we would be facing each game. After graduating, I spent many years coaching in Little League as well as at the high school level. My background taught me that, during a game, there were times when it was possible to determine the type of pitch the pitcher was going to throw to the batter. At the Little League level, this was easy. Each pitch would be a soft lob which, if the prevailing winds were favorable, might make it to the plate. However, as the players progressed in levels and skills, the pitcher would likely have a variety of pitches ranging from a fastball to a change-up, to a slider, to a curve. Each of those pitches might have several variations. It is always of great advantage to the hitters to know what type of pitch might be coming to the plate.

As an adult living in the Northwest, I have seen Randy Johnson, a pitcher formerly of the Seattle Mariners baseball team, create fear within a batter. Presently, Randy is one of the best pitchers in professional baseball. He throws the ball at around 95-98 miles per hour. This is very scary for hitters, especially if they had expected a slow, looping curve ball and instead, received a fastball buzzing by their chest at 95 miles per hour. Randy's ability to vary his pitches confuses the hitters, and lends to his remarkable success as a pitcher. If all he threw were fastballs down the middle of the plate, the hitters would do much better against him.

Telegraphing the "Pitch"

One aspect of my coaching was to look for little flaws in the pitcher's delivery. Did the pitcher kick his leg higher

on a fastball? Was his glove more open when he pitched a curve ball? Was his arm lower when he threw a slider? This is called "telegraphing a pitch." This allows the batter to anticipate more accurately what type of pitch is thrown from the pitcher's hand. Imagine the relief of knowing the kind of pitch that is coming to the plate. All the guesswork is gone and the batter can concentrate on one thing—hitting the ball.

Unfortunately, people who violate others with their reports (remember these people are "us") don't carry huge signs saying, "Beware! Carrier of false report!" or, "Here comes an evil report." Nor do they respond as the lepers did in the Old Testament by shouting "Unclean, unclean!" It would be glorious if we had such obvious warnings in preparation for evil reports. As with many successful pitchers, these people "mix up" or "vary" their approach, making the awareness of what pitch is coming difficult to ascertain. The result is often confusion for the recipient of the report.

However, I do believe there are some key indicators which let us know what "pitch" is coming. Fortunately, they often "telegraph" their pitch. Let's examine some methods of "delivering" an evil report. Being aware of these can help prevent us from being "duped" or "taken in" by their apparently "sincere desire" to just talk and share their heart. In this particular case, the posture of "Don't be upset with me, I am just the messenger," does not apply, because it is the messenger (as well as the message) that may be on the brink of violating our spirit.

How do we identify the messenger who carries these defiling attitudes and conversations? Let's examine eight tactics (or strategies) used by those who are messengers of defiling information. By knowing these areas, it will help us to ferret out the motives of the speaker and thereby protect our spirits from violation and defilement.

Identifying Actions of Evil Reporters

1. Does the messenger look for support from you for their beliefs, attitudes and/or actions expressed in their conversation? Do you find yourself with a sympathetic spirit regarding their situation or the person's expressed scenario?

What signals do you give off? Do you raise your eyebrows in interest? Does your body language say, "I want to hear this?" Do you say, "Let me hear more?"

The Bible shares a story, found in the Book of Esther, about a man named Haman, who gave an evil report. Esther, of Hebrew descent, was queen of the land. However, her lineage was unknown to the king. Her Uncle Mordecai was a faithful Hebrew man. Haman, an officer in the king's court, was placed in charge over the people by the king. Haman wanted Mordecai to bow down and acknowledge his authority, which Mordecai refused to do. Angered and full of jealousy, Haman approached the king.

> *Then Haman said to King Ahasuerus, "There is a certain people scattered and dispersed among the people in all the provinces of your kingdom; their laws are different from all other peoples, and they do not keep the king's laws. Therefore it is not fitting for the king to let them remain. If it pleases the king, let a decree be written that they be destroyed, and I will pay ten thousand talents of silver into the hands of those who do the work, to bring it into the king's treasuries."*
>
> Esth. 3:8, 9

The king's response was to give his signet ring to Haman to validate the decree. Haman must have tested the king's spirit many times, for he knew the king would respond in pride and jealousy. There is no indication of the king's questioning Haman's report. The response of the king was of total acceptance. Haman "tipped off his pitch," but the king missed the opportunity to recognize what was happening at the time. The king was so interested in supporting Haman and acknowledging the authority which was placed upon Haman that he did not question Haman's actions.

It is very common for us to allow a person to discuss an area without questioning them. We, often times, want to "support them" because they are a friend, supervisor or person with influence. The reason the messenger came to you may have been that they knew you would not disagree with or question them. Are we being used by these people because of our own gullibility and blindness to negative speech patterns?

2. Messengers with an evil report will try to distract you from your present focus or course of action. In Nehemiah, chapter six, this method was used in an attempt to dissuade Nehemiah from rebuilding the walls of Jerusalem. Four times his enemies sent someone to distract Nehemiah; four times he refused to quit working and leave the work on the wall. A fifth distraction occurred when a letter was taken to Nehemiah alleging that the Jewish people and Nehemiah were planning a rebellion. However, Nehemiah did not take the bait. He refused to entertain their distractions. In chapter 6, verse 10, we find Nehemiah is approached for a sixth time. *"...Shemaiah said, 'Let us meet together in the house of God, within the temple, and let us close the doors of the temple, for they are coming to kill you, and they are coming to kill you at night.'"* It is here that we see the evil report being presented in an attempt to garner an emotional response from Nehemiah. Will he respond with, "Why would they do that?" or, "Who are these people?" In verse 11, Nehemiah says, *"But I said, 'Should a man like me flee? And could one such as I go into the temple to save his life? I will not go in.'"* It was Nehemiah's refusal to engage the evil report that allowed him to receive insight from God. *"Then I perceived that surely God had not sent him...He was* *hired for this reason, that I might become frightened and act accordingly and sin, so that they might have an evil report in order that they could reproach me"*(v. 12-13). Nehemiah recognized the indicators given off by the transgressor and was able to avoid the entanglement of the enemy.

3. The transporter of a false report will attempt to create disunity and division among people. The Pharisees commonly used this method by trying to separate the people from Jesus. Their emphasis was to show the people, or their leaders, how Jesus was blasphemous, sacrilegious or a violator of the Word of God. Phrases like, "Wait until I tell you about the adulterous woman!" and "Have you heard the blasphemy he uttered?" were being spewed forth from their lips daily. If the listeners had not been on guard, curiosity would have quickly taken over and they would have been caught in a trap of listening to an evil report. *"The pitcher looks at homeplate; he winds up; here comes the pitch..."* We need to be prepared for the traps of the enemy. First Peter 5:8 speaks clearly in warning us to beware of Satan and his traps, *"Be sober, be vigilant; because your adversary the devil walks about like a roaring lion, seeking whom he may devour."*

Each one of us should be guarding our spirits and be on the lookout for times when we might be susceptible to an evil report from a messenger. The fact is, the world is full of these types of discussions and therefore, we should anticipate the possibility of listening to negative comments. It would behoove us to think of ways to avoid these traps (discussed later in this book) and to put on the armor of God prior to going into some of the common areas of defilement (school, work, church).

4. An individual who conveys negative reports often shows anger when you disagree with them. One way to determine the motives of the individual who is sharing a report is to watch his or her reaction when you disagree with the individual. Anger or defensiveness are obvious signs that the person is not looking for guidance and direction, but has an emotional investment and a desire to gain support for his or her "side of the story." Imagine the response from Judas when Jesus did not support the hoarding of oil and allowed it to be used for the anointing of his feet.

> *Then Mary took a pound of very costly oil of spikenard, anointed the feet of Jesus, and wiped His feet with her hair. And the house was filled with the fragrance of the oil. But one of His disciples, Judas Iscariot, Simon's son, who would betray Him, said, "Why was this fragrant oil not sold for three hundred denarii and given to the poor?" This he said, not that he cared for the poor, but because he was a thief, and had the moneybox; and he used to take what was put in it. But Jesus said, "Let her alone she has kept this for the day of My burial. For the poor you have with you always, but Me you do not have always"*
>
> John 12:3-6

Ironically, in the next chapter of John, we read about Jesus identifying His betrayer. No doubt, Judas was angry at being rebuffed by Jesus. Our Lord Jesus Christ knew the consequences of listening to an evil report.

5. A messenger sharing information that will violate your spirit will often approach with an apparently demure and modest attitude. They appear to need your advice and guidance, portraying themselves as being unable to "figure it out." This is very common for the experienced carrier of an evil report. "Could I ask your opinion on something?" While this may sound innocent and innocuous, after we reply "Yes," a statement such as this may follow: "Yesterday Jenny did something really awful. She went to this movie and...."

Simple questions are used to draw us into the conversation, often by tapping into our curiosity. Let me share some quick, helpful responses for those questions that cause us problems.

Question: "Can you keep a secret?" Response: "Not really."

Question: "Did you hear about Carol?" Response: "Yes, isn't she a sweet person?"

Question: "Wait until you hear about Tim." Response: "Okay, I'll wait. Thanks."

Our curiosity becomes aroused and before we know it, we have listened to an evil report about Jenny. This "messenger of pain" did not really want any advice or guidance. If we were to ask them why they told us about the incident, their reply might be that they weren't sure if they should do something about the incident or tell someone about it. HELLO! It appears this person decided to use us as their little "testing ground." Defilement comes in subtle and quick ways, if we are not protecting our spirits.

> *Then Sanballat sent his servant to me as before, the fifth time, with an open letter in hand. In it was written: It is reported among the nations, and Geshem says, that you and the Jews plan to rebel; therefore, according to these rumors, you are rebuilding the wall, that you may be their king. And you have also appointed prophets to proclaim concerning you at Jerusalem, saying, "There is a king in Judah!" Now these matters will be reported to the king. So come, therefore, and let us consult together.*
>
> Neh. 6:5-7

Nehemiah emphasizes that carriers of evil reports do not stop after one attempt. If one pitch doesn't work, then lookout! Here comes another one!

They were asking Nehemiah "for counsel," "wisdom," and "guidance" in solving their so-called problem. Did Nehemiah take the bait? Did he fall for this trap and agree to meet with them? We read his response in verse eight, *"Then I sent to him, saying, 'No such things as you say are being done, but you invent them in your own heart.'"* Nehemiah was able to see what was coming. The carrier of the report "telegraphed his pitch" and Nehemiah refused to receive it.

6. A transporter of negative information will attempt to show off their power, strength or authority. Due to the nature of their jobs, whom they know, or by being in the right place at the right time, some people are able to gain advancement in the eyes of the world. These people build their houses on sand. In other words, they look for continued worldly encouragement based on a temporary whimsical moment of recognition. It is common for them to take advantage of this by "showing off" their newly found authority. Be on the look out for this type of insecurity in people. This is a possible sign that information which will violate your spirit may be forthcoming.

These types of people may use their information as a power base. They may have more knowledge than the "average" person, so that the carrier uses their newly found knowledge as a lure. The sinful nature of man opens up areas of temptation. Many people see knowledge as translating to power. The sinful nature of man still has a pull toward having power in his life. The temptation of Jesus, found in Matthew four, is a classic example of this type of approach.

> *Again, the devil took Him up on an exceedingly high mountain, and showed Him all the kingdoms of the world and their glory. And he said to Him, "All these things I will give You if You will fall down and worship me."*
>
> Matt. 4:8, 9

Satan tries to tempt us with the enticing aspects of power, riches and recognition. The carrier of an evil report uses his/her position of knowledge to attract us and place us in a position to stumble.

7. The individual will flatter you and praise you. Think back to the last time that someone spoke flattering words to you. (If you can't remember, that may be a good sign.) It is common for people who want something or desire to influence your thinking to use compliments as a way to set up their approach. After someone gives a compliment, a typical response might be, "Okay, what do you want?" How about when your children said, "You are the best mom in the world" which is quickly followed by "Can I have a dollar to go to the store?" This is not to suggest that every compliment is intended to manipulate your  emotions. There are many times when people sincerely give words of praise simply to encourage a person. I desire to compliment and praise my wife and children as a source of strength and love. However, flattery is also a tool one may utilize when attempting to manipulate and deposit an evil report within another person. Praise or flattery prepares a person to receive the report as it creates a more receptive spirit within an individual.

There is an armed forces approach that employs the strategy of using military power (troops, artillery, bombs) to wear down the enemy prior to a big strike. This is referred to as "softening the enemy." People will use words to "soften us up" before they come at us with a larger attack. They prey upon our pride, insecurity and desire for recognition. After all, if a person thinks I have great ideas and is simply asking for my perspective, why shouldn't I listen to them and then give them feedback? The reason is that by listening I will become polluted and my perceptions will become distorted. *"...Therefore do not associate with one who flatters with his lips"*(Prov. 20:19b).

8. The messenger of an evil report will often embellish and exaggerate a situation to make it seem far worse than it really is. In Numbers 13, God told Moses to send out people into the land of Canaan to spy out the land.

*"And the Lord spoke to Moses, saying, 'Send men to spy out the land of Canaan, which **I am giving** to the children of Israel.'"* Notice there was not a question as to whether they should invade the land of Canaan. God had already stated that He was giving it to them. However, ten of those spies came back with an evil report. They became detectives of darkness, exaggerating and evoking wild imaginations among the people.

> *And they gave the children of Israel a **bad report** of the land which they had spied out, saying, "The land through which we have gone as spies is a land that devours its inhabitants, and all the people whom we saw in it are men of great stature. There we saw the*

giants; and we were like grasshoppers in our own sight, so we were in their sight."

Num. 13:32, 33

The people of Israel listened, became frightened and departed from their faith in God. This is exactly what happens when we listen to evil reports. Our carnal minds take over and overwhelm our spirit of faith. Suddenly, what was within the realm of possibility in God is now impossible even to imagine.

These eight areas create an atmosphere of confusion, disloyalty, terror and fear. Remember, if we are on the alert, we can foresee the pitch of the enemy coming toward us. We can choose not to receive it. Proverbs 11:9 says, *"Dishonest people use gossip to destroy their neighbors; good people are protected by their own good sense"*(Common English Version). We all need to pray and ask for God's wisdom, so we can be protected with "good sense."

QUESTION—Examining the Heart

1. Are you able to think of one person whom you would identify as a "carrier of evil reports"?

2. What is the impact upon you, when this type of person begins to share negative reports?

INITIAL RESPONSES TO AN EVIL REPORT

CHAPTER 3

INITIAL RESPONSES TO AN EVIL REPORT

Many of us may now begin to see multiple times we have been caught or trapped in the scenario of listening to an evil report. We may get surprised and find ourselves listening to a conversation before realizing what has happened to us. It is important not to be too harsh on ourselves when this happens. We must begin to change habit patterns and develop new listening skills. Our focus must change and we are to have our antennas up and be prepared for negative comments and subtle innuendoes about people. This would be especially true when we find ourselves with certain people or in specific situations that, in the past, have been filled with defiling conversations.

I was recently at a family gathering with some relatives. As in the past, the conversation began to turn to negative talk and gossip surrounding people. I made a comment regarding the negative nature of the conversation. This did not dissuade anyone and the negative tone continued. Again, I made a comment about not speaking negatively about others. While I was not about to win any popularity contests, it did get my point across. For the next few days, when the conversation leaned toward gossip, they would look at me and make a comment like, "We better not say anything bad or Mike will tell us to stop." I didn't mind this at all. In fact, it only encouraged me to "draw the line" a little sooner in future conversations.

Remember, people don't usually get caught up in sin without prior warning. Adultery, fornication, lying, cheating and other areas of sin often occur by a slow seduction of our flesh and mind. If we allow these strongholds to permeate our thoughts and emotions, we will be deceived. Once we are aware of the patterns of our life and those of the world, we can begin to be pro-active and prevent falling into temptation.

I read a little story that talks about the patterns and habits of life. It reminded me of the traps we fall into regarding negative reports.

Chapter 1—"I walk down the street. There is a deep hole in the sidewalk and I fall in. I am lost...I am helpless. It isn't my fault. It takes forever to find a way out."

Chapter 2—"I walk down the same street. There is a deep hole in the sidewalk. I pretend I don't see it. I fall in, again. I can't believe I am in this same place. But, it isn't my fault. It still takes a long time to get out."

Chapter 3—"I walk down the same street. There is a deep hole in the sidewalk. I see it is there. I still fall in...it is a habit...But, my eyes are open. I know where I am. It is my fault. I get out immediately."

Chapter 4—"I walk down the same street. There is a deep hole in the sidewalk. I walk around it."

Chapter 5—"I walk down another street."

(author unknown)

This story illustrates the tendency to develop a repetitive cycle of sin in a life via habit patterns. We can begin to overcome these areas and prevent them from occurring by our willingness to learn new patterns. Chapter one of this book allowed us to formalize a definition for an evil report. Now I would like to expand on your understanding of evil reports. Let me remind you of the first definition and then include an additional definition.

An individual, maliciously, using words or attitude, causes injury, damage or discredit to another's reputation or character. (first definition)

An unauthorized, distorted or false report which influences us to form an evil opinion about another person. **(new definition)**

Let's start with an actual day in your life. You are sitting at work, home, school or church, minding your own business (naturally) and being very spiritual. Suddenly, out of the blue, Clarissa says, "Did you hear about William?" As a natural (and habitual) response, you say, "No, what?" She begins to talk, a red flag is sent up, sirens begin to go off in your mind, a little voice says, "Warning, Warning, Danger Ahead!" What do you say? Can you simply walk away? It is so common for us to feel trapped and therefore allow people to continue in their conversation, even if we feel defiled and uncomfortable. The ensuing pages explore different ways to examine the motives and intentions of a person *before* we listen to their full report. We can begin to train our mind and our response patterns to discourage certain types of conversations, narrowing the chances of our listening to a false report. By directing questions and statements to the carrier of the evil report, we demand clarification and a thoughtful response. This will allow those who are desiring to be godly not to violate another person through murmuring and to check their own spirit and, perhaps, stop from slandering another individual.

My youngest son, Luke, was listening to my wife and me discuss this book. Joyce was asking for some clarification in an effort to help focus some of my thought patterns. Luke interrupted us and said, "If someone is telling you something bad about another person all you need to do is turn to them and say, 'Gossip, gossip, gossip, gossip!'" After my wife and I stopped laughing, I realized that was actually a pretty good strategy. I'm sure it would cut off the conversation quickly. But, just in case you are not as bold as my son, the following questions and statements are practical and easy to utilize in the midst of conversations.

Questions to Ask

1. "Is this something I need to hear about?" This question asks the person to substantiate the legitimacy of telling *you*. While it may be important for someone to know the information, are you the one who should be told?

The person may respond with a hesitant, "Well, I'm not

sure." Ask them to think about it further before sharing any more with you. This comment will help a person, who is unknowingly about to be involved in gossip. The purpose of this question is to prevent people from sharing gossip as a part of their habit patterns.

I was recently in a counseling session with a man who was separated from his wife. We were preparing for a reconciliation meeting. At one point, he said, "You probably don't know this about Karen, but when she was younger..."

I immediately interrupted him and said, "Terry, if Karen hasn't told me, then I don't want to hear it from you." He agreed and we went on with the rest of the session. If it had been critical, Terry could have brought it up with Karen in the room. It is common to find "Christians" who know gossip and murmuring is wrong, yet still are parties to both. This is especially true when someone is hurt or angry. When confronted, they admit they don't like it, but it is "such a bad habit." Your gentle, yet firm approach can help break this pattern.

2. "What specific parts of this conversation need to be discussed with me?" This type of question is a little more confrontational, but still gives the person an opportunity to gain control of their tongue. It challenges the individual to not take me through a ten-minute scenario before getting to the actual point of their story. If the individual will speak to the main points of the issue and cut out the extraneous parts, the listener does not need to dissect the story, cutting away the negative and biased comments. Remember, by listening to the person, we indirectly support and encourage them to continue to share the information.

Will a person ever become offended or upset by being asked these questions? Possibly, but what may seem like an offense might actually be the conviction of the Lord. Again, don't be a party to an evil report. There are *repercussions to sin* and **listening to an evil report is a sin**, as Nebuchadnezzar found out. God speaks clearly about those who are apostates, or who renounce their belief in God. The Book of Jude says, *"These are grumblers, complainers, walking according to their own lusts; and they mouth great swelling words, flattering people to gain advantage"* (Jude 16). Never let it be that our actions and/or words show us to be deserters of the faith. We need to guard our actions and words in order to maintain a strong, personal relationship with Jesus Christ.

My prayer for all of us would be, *"Oh Lord, allow our lips to be pure before You. Allow our ears to hear only that which edifies the body of Christ and keeps us holy. When hearing of misfortune or the "fall" of a brother or sister, let our desire be to pray for them, to ask Your Holy Spirit to convict them and to restore them. Father God, keep us protected from the adversary and his devious ways. Bring to our minds and to our spirits, the strength to turn away from evil and run into Your loving arms. Amen."*

3. "I am going to take notes so I can recall details, do you mind?" This statement and question may cause a tremendous uneasiness in the transmitter of a negative report. People don't like to be held accountable for their stories and murmuring. It is very common that at this point, the person changes their story and their tact with you. It was during one counseling session that an individual began to say negative things about another person in the church. I took out a notepad and said, "Please continue, I just want to be sure I hear you correctly so we can sit down with this sister and work through a Matthew 18 process."

At this point, the individual stopped and said, "Well, I probably shouldn't say anything else until I talk with this other person." AMEN! There is something about putting words in writing that makes people hesitate and puts fear in people. (We call it accountability.)

4. "Who told you this information?" This is a critical question to ask people. Once again, you are calling them to accountability. I can just hear someone respond, "I am not supposed to tell." Oh really! When one refuses to identify the source of the information, it is a sure sign of hiddenness, secrecy and a potentially evil report. Many times, it is almost impossible to track down the original source of false reports. Do you remember the activity game called "Telephone?" Ten to fifteen people stand in a circle. One person whispers a statement into the ear of the person next to him and then that person quietly whispers the comment to the next person. The phrase or story is passed from person to person. Most often, a key word or portion of the story is inadvertently left out, mostly due to poor or selective listening. When the last person hears the story and then it is shared with the others, it is usually much different than its original form. "Telephone" is humorous because it is a game. In reality, distorted facts and story changes where "truth becomes stranger than fiction" can be deadly. Do not be a part of this cycle. Refuse to be a listener of an evil report.

5. "Is this your opinion/interpretation of something you have heard or did you observe this situation?" Remember the definition shared earlier in this chapter, *"An unauthorized, distorted or false report which influences us* *to form an evil opinion about another person."* It is possible to share facts and yet misrepresent them due to the essence (or nature) of our hearts. We see this in the advertising and marketing business. A portion of the facts (or only favorable facts) become known to the consumer. This changes the perception of the product being presented to the public. In the case of an evil report, you are the consumer. The person sharing a report with you may only tell you a portion of the situation. They may taint the story with facial expressions, body language and little comments which influence your receptivity to the information.

All evil reports are not necessarily false reports. *"Did you hear about James and Tonya? They got into a really big argument and talked about getting a divorce. And to think he is an elder in the church and she is part of the Sunday school ministry. How can they get a divorce and call themselves Christians?"* The truth of the situation is James and Tonya had an argument and the comment "maybe we should have never gotten married" or even, "we'd be better off divorced" was said. What was not reported was that they went to their pastor, asked for prayer, repented for their rebellion toward one another, and agreed to continue godly counsel. True, some of the harsh words should not have been spoken, but their response was far from what was reported to have taken place. Whether the report is true or false, it still can be an evil report. Having the "reporter" check out the validity and the facts of the situation will prevent the spreading of rumors.

It is imperative to ask questions and make statements about your impression when listening to a person. Like a runaway train, our lips can get going and easily get "derailed." If the situation is one that the person observed, or was a part of, there are the elements of emotions, hurts, confusion and perception that must be addressed. If the situation is one which was passed on to them by another, we certainly must consider that the person sharing the story may have been distorting the facts and perceived something other than the factual occurrences.

6. "May I quote you after I check this out?" Those who give an evil report often claim to be misquoted. How many times do we see this in the newspaper? "The senator is a cheating, lying politician who should never be trusted..." says his political opponent. The next day we read, "The political opponent says he was misquoted and the information was taken out of context." Naturally, the initial report is on the front page while the retraction or clarification is on the fourteenth page. Stating that I was misquoted is a way to avoid admitting to giving a false report. I neither accept responsibility nor do I need to ask for forgiveness.

Asking a person if they object to being quoted creates a depth of accountability for their words. In order to protect himself, the evil reporter might say, "Oh no! Don't quote me. It would hurt their feelings if they knew I told you." or, "They would be mad at me." If a person is unwilling to stand up for what he or she said, something is amiss.

7. "Before you share any further, what are you expecting from me?" This will help clarify the ground rules of the conversation. Through this question, we want to know the purpose behind the sharing of information and what they are expecting from us. Is it to receive prayer? Is it to get counsel and guidance? Is it to spread gossip and slander? (Bingo!)

When I taught sixth grade, gossip (or tattling) was a common problem. During recess, a child would come and complain that someone took the basketball or another person pushed him or her down. This often resulted in students being separated or being reprimanded. It was on a cold, snowy day that I understood, for the first time, the manipulation taking place from these chronic tattlers. On this day, Carol told me about José throwing a snowball. I was cold, distracted and decided to dismiss it as a minor incident. However, Carol responded by asking me, "Aren't you going to do anything?"

My retort was clear and precise, "What would you like me to do?"

Carol said, "He should be in trouble and miss recess. That's what always happens when I tell the teachers about José."

Carol had her mind made up as to what her expectations were from me. If these expectations were not met, arguing, complaining and whining were sure to follow. From then on, prior to giving any answers, I would ask Carol, "What are you expecting from me?" or "What kind of answer will satisfy you?" This approach helps to get covert agendas placed on top instead of having them underneath the table.

8. "Do you agree (or find validity) with this situation as it has been presented to you?" I like to personalize the problem and have the individual analyze it biblically. Is the incident consistent with what one knows about the people involved? Are we looking for a solution? Ask the person what the Bible says about the issues; how would Jesus handle the problem; what can be done to help those involved? They may ask for your impressions of the situation. This gives you an excellent opportunity to respond with, "It probably is something the people involved in need to pray about and get guidance from God." or, "It really doesn't matter what I think since it has nothing to do with me." Or even, "I think we need to pray for them right now, will you join me?"

9. "Have you spoken to those people who are directly involved with this situation?" If someone is concerned about another person, or if an individual is upset with another, the Bible is very clear about the procedure that should be followed. In Matthew 18:15, it says, *"Moreover if your brother sins against you, go and tell him his fault between you and him alone. If he hears you, you have gained your brother..."* We must begin to approach one another in love in an effort to restore our brothers and sisters. Spirituality is not measured by how well we expose an offender, but by how effectively we restore an offender.

> *Brethren, if a man is overtaken (or caught) in any trespass, you who are spiritual restore such a one in a spirit of gentleness, considering yourself lest you also be tempted. Bear one another's burdens, and so fulfill the law of Christ.*
>
> Gal 6:1, 2

I like the way this scripture is written in the Contemporary English Version:

> *My friends, you are spiritual. So if someone is trapped in sin, you should gently lead that person back to the right path. But watch out, and don't be tempted yourself. You obey the law of Christ when you offer each other a helping hand.*

It is very clear from this scripture that we are to help restore an individual, not uncover them. While some of us want to believe we have a *"Gift of Exposing,"* we should seek the *"Ministry of Restoration."*

We read the story of Noah in the Book of Genesis. One

night, he became drunk and lay naked (or uncovered) in his tent. One of his sons, Ham, saw this and went to tell his brothers. Can you imagine the conversation? "Hey, guys, guess what? Dad is drunk and doesn't have any clothes on." The brothers, Shem and Japheth, responded by taking a garment, walking in backwards and covering their father. What Noah did was wrong, but it did not need to be exposed (no pun intended) to other people. He needed to be restored. What Ham intended as an evil report was dealt with in a godly fashion. As a result, Noah trusted Shem and Japheth and blessed them.

10. "It is important for me to pray about this (or get counsel from leadership) before I respond to you." This is an excellent way to model to the person that you are not about to make a quick decision, or respond emotionally. Often, the situation being discussed will affect you personally. This is why they have chosen you to share the scenario. However, by guarding your emotions and your personal response, you will prevent yourself from becoming emotionally entangled, thus opening your spirit up to a spiritual attack. When in doubt, pray. When unsure, pray. When confused, pray. God is truly asking us to lean on Him for all situations. I don't want people to receive "my counsel"; I want to give them the *mind of the Lord*. The only way to do this is by being in prayer and seeking God in my personal life.

The above questions and statements help each person gain a better understanding of the motivation of the reporter. The reporter may ask us **to pray** for the person. They may be wanting to inform us because of a position we are in **to help, aid or support** them. It could be **to get counsel** from us as to how a situation should be handled. These are but a few *legitimate reasons* to share situations.

Look at the attitude, the tonal expressions and facial features. Hear not only what people are saying, but how they are saying it. We have often heard how bad it is to gossip or give an evil report, but seldom do we realize the damage done to our spirit by even listening to an evil report. We must not be ignorant to what constitutes an evil report and how it is given. In the next section, we will address the aspect of **"confusion"** and how it impacts our walk with Christ.

QUESTIONS—Examining the Heart

1. Do you remember ever utilizing any questions and/or statements when hearing an evil report? If yes, how did the situation work out?

2. What would be the most difficult part of using the suggested strategies?

3. Would it be easier to use the strategies with a friend? A stranger?

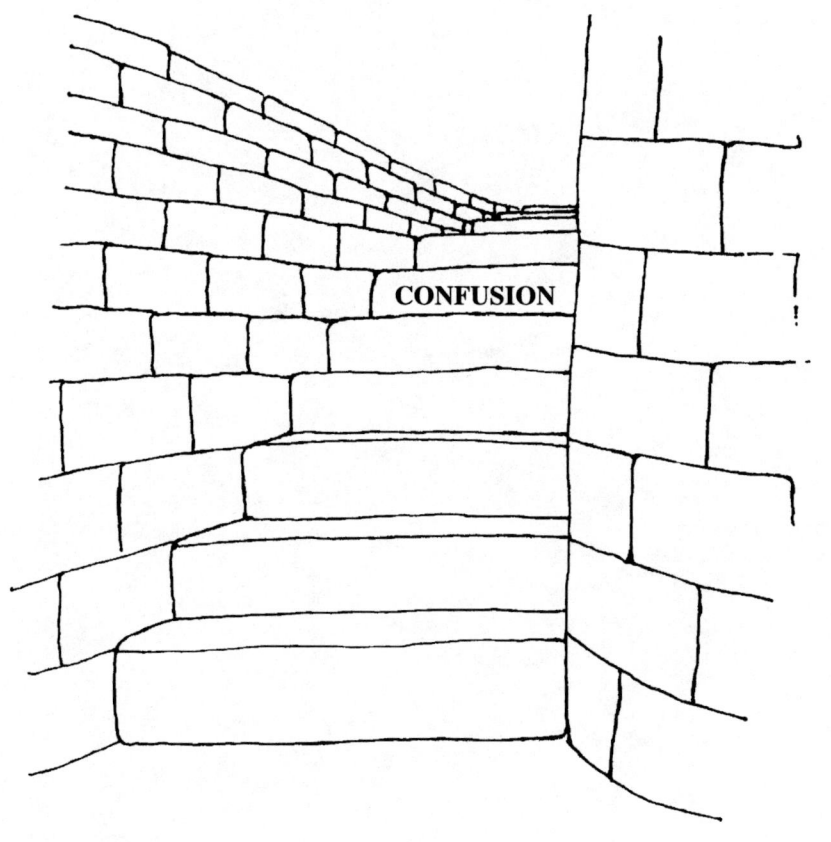

CHAPTER 4

CONFUSION

I believe there are many layers and stairsteps that progressively lead an individual into a place of deception. The importance of recognizing the subtle defilement of our mind and spirit when listening to an evil report is essential in our Christian life. There are many reasons we allow our ears to listen to impure words and our eyes to view impure actions. There may be pressure from colleagues, family or friends. We may feel trapped by circumstances or situations and feel unable to "take a stand" toward righteousness. We may be rebellious and make a conscious decision to violate the ways of God. There are those who think they are "strong enough" to see and hear such things, but not let those things affect them. This apparent display of individual strength undermines the authority of God in our lives.

A major factor for allowing negative words and actions to violate our sense of well-being is found under the category of **confusion.** This is the specific area we will focus on for the next few pages. Confusion is a major stumbling block to our progressing in our walk with Christ. *"In thee, O Lord, do I put my trust; let me never be put to confusion"* (Ps. 71:1, KJV). Yes, confusion can be a major reason for our sinful ways. One of the greatest tools Satan uses is confusion. The more people become confused, the greater the chance they will make foolish decisions and become contaminated. God's desire is for us to increase in knowledge and be wise as to the ways of the enemy. *"The heart of the prudent acquires knowledge, And the ear of the wise seeks knowledge"* (Prov. 18:15).

CONFUSION: Listening to conflicting voices and refusing to submit to the one of higher authority.

Imagine that an onion is placed in front of you. Before you begin to cry, let's imagine that it is a "tearless" onion. (We can only wish for such a blessing.) Take this onion and begin to peel it by hand. Each time you take a layer off the onion, another layer is found below the skin. This will continue until the layers are gone and the heart or core of the onion is revealed. Confusion is the same thing. There are many layers to it, but there will eventually be an exposed core. We will begin to examine the different layers of confusion in an effort to "expose the core" so God can purify the heart of each one of us.

Layers of Confusion

A. When we are involved in the area of **"confusion," we lose sight of what is really important in our lives.** My wife, Joyce, and I are the best of friends. We feel very comfortable in sharing our personal dreams and desires with one another. Our marriage is wonderful, and I feel there is no other couple as happy or as blessed as we are in life. (I am not so naive as to believe we don't have problems or struggles, but we are committed to working our issues out. Many years ago we agreed that divorce was *not* an option in our marriage. My lovely wife is stuck with me. I am, among men, most richly blessed.) Despite our commitment and covenant pledge "to honor, obey, love and encourage," there are times when we become "confused" emotionally and our conversations become negative and we contaminate one another.

My role as a husband involves helping with the laundry, transporting our sons to activities, providing financial security, helping with homework, maintaining a strong spiritual climate in the house...among other areas. Joyce and I are a team and we work together in life.

One area which I have "helped" with for many years is doing dishes. At times, I have felt that "the family" did not do as good a job of cleaning the dishes as they should have done, so I have become the resident dishwasher. (In our house the dishwasher is not automatic. Although, when I get in sync and find a rhythm, I hum right along.) This is not a job or chore I resent, but one which I feel I can be of help to my wife.

However, there are times when I am doing this satisfying area of servanthood with a tremendous heart of love (of course) and my words begin to contradict my actions.

"Why can't you clean the dishes like this?" or, "If you would just rinse off all the soap, it is so much simpler." These words place a barrier between us and injure our relationship. This is especially true when there are other people around to hear my words of "encouragement." Praise God for His forgiveness and grace over my insensitive nature. I can't imagine living a life without Christ's conviction and an avenue for coming to the foot of the Cross for repentance.

Confusion causes a blindness in our lives. We begin to say negative comments which cause injury to those around us. Our insensitivity is seen by our tactlessness about when to say something and when to keep our mouths shut. Instead of sitting down with my wife and sharing privately the concerns I may have, I have at times used public opportunities to slander and injure the one I love. We must be careful with our words, they can cause serious damage to relationships.

B. "Confusion" impacts those around us and creates disorder in life. This infectious nature of confusion is seen when Gideon destroyed the Midianites and Amalekites (Judg. 7). Gideon and his three hundred men were strategically placed around the camp of the enemy.

> *Now the Midianites and Amalekites, all the people of the East, were lying in the valley as numerous as locusts; and their camels were without number, as the sand by the seashore in multitude. Then Gideon divided the three hundred men into three companies, and he put a trumpet into every man's hand, with empty pitchers, and torches inside the pitchers.*
>
> Judg. 7:12, 16

The army of God waited for the signal from Gideon. They

blew their trumpets, broke the pitchers and held up torches. The Bible tells us that the enemies of God were so "confused," they began to attack one another. So great was the confusion, that disorder and disunity occurred, and the Midianites and Amalekites killed one another. I can just imagine it. One person yells, "What is going on?"

Another soldier says, "Look out, I see torches and hear the horns of battle."

One soldier sees a sword being pulled out, in the dark of night. The glint of the moonlight off the sword's sharp edge quickens his pulse. He must defend himself! "What is happening? Why is there so much noise? Those trumpets are deafening; the torches are coming at us...I need to attack before I am slain!" Quickly, without hesitation, he thrusts his sword in the nearest person. Within a moment of time, the soldiers are fighting shadows and movements. Get the picture? It is pretty easy to see how this confusion becomes rampant in the camp of the enemy.

It is exactly like that in our lives. When we become confused, we allow ourselves to be impacted by those around us. Our own thoughts and feelings become subject to the influences of those around us. It has been said that we are known by the company we keep. If we surround ourselves with people who are seeking God, walking in an upright manner, our lives will reflect this condition. If we keep company with those who gossip, murmur and are discontented, our spirits will be defiled, and we will be a reflection of this attitude.

It is imperative that when one is counseling, evangelizing, discipling or involved in any other type of ministry, we put on the armor of God. Whenever I pray for someone in the area of deliverance from bondage, spiritual oppression or demonic spirits (depression, infirmity, etc.),

I always pray a cleansing prayer over all of those involved in the prayer time. The nature of confusion is too easily imparted to one another. This is especially true when a situation is somewhat stressful or volatile. How many times have we read in a newspaper about the end of a football game where players were unsure as to what play was to be run, the coaching staff was confused, therefore, the result was defeat?

What about on the political front? Those in political office often attribute errors in statements and decisions to confusion among their staff, political antagonists, or among the general public. Conflicting statements abound and it is difficult to decipher truth from deception. Confusion opens up our body, soul and spirit to be influenced by the environment around us.

An individual called and asked to meet with me regarding some dreams and nightmares she had been tormented by over recent weeks. My wife and I met with her and she shared a series of bizarre events in her life which had opened up many demonic doors. We listened, gave counsel and then prayed over her for quite some time. Honestly, it was a rather strange situation. While my wife and I felt confident in our prayers and the authority which God has given to all of us (Mark 16)—this particular time of counsel and prayer was filled with conflicting stories and disjointed thought patterns. That night, both Joyce and I felt defiled, unclean and oppressed, as if a spirit was coming against us. We realized we had not cleansed ourselves after meeting with that person. It was very apparent to us that some of those spirits and oppressive tendencies had attached themselves to us. That is, we had become contaminated by the ungodly conversation.

We spent some time in prayer, broke strongholds in our

lives and closed open doors which received the oppressive spirits and words. The oppression lifted and we learned a valuable lesson. The Bible states that spirits are looking for a place to inhabit. If we are not careful, we can pick up other people's offenses, attitudes, feelings of anger or jealousy, or even their unclean spirits. Protect yourself by covering up with the armor of God.

I became a Christian in 1977. I moved to a small town in Northern Idaho and was part of a program called VISTA (Volunteers In Service To America). My desire to serve and help others was great, but my foundation of servanthood was weak. I became friends with a young man named Tom. He and I would play basketball together, go to movies and "hang out." Of course, part of his "hanging out" included going to the bars to drink beer. I was a new Christian and still had many "marks of the world" on me. I had not placed myself in a position of being discipled by a godly person nor was I involved in accountability with other Christian brothers, so I was unsure in many foundational areas of Christianity. I accompanied Tom to the bar and inevitably spent time drinking.

After a period of time, God showed me the poor testimony this presented to those around me. I was known as Tom's drinking buddy, not as a man who loved God. This type of compromise is common among the Christian community. I felt a conviction from the Holy Spirit, but in my immaturity and confusion, was unsure what it meant. I quit drinking beer, began drinking soda pop, but still I remained within the bar setting.

Again, God convicted me of partaking in the coarse, crude jokes and fellowship found in most bars. I told Tom that I could no longer accompany him to the bars. As I look back on that time, I realize my relationship with Tom began to deteriorate after that incident, and it was the beginning of the end for our apparent friendship.

I do not blame Tom for what happened. This was my error and my sin. A lack of discipline and the failure to place myself under godly headship resulted in my wanting to touch the Spirit of God *and* the spirits of the world. Due to the lack of strong accountability and discipling, my testimony and impact in that town were minimal. Sadly enough, people would only remember me as a guy who would go to the bars, listen to crude jokes *and drink a coke*. I praise God for His revelation in my life and the importance of knowing the type of influence people have on one another.

It was very apparent to me in subsequent years, that God wanted me to be a pure vessel for Him to use. My confusion was due to immaturity and a lack of receiving teaching from godly people. Unfortunately, I influenced many people during that time in my life. There were many men and women who wanted to know more about God and looked to me as a role model of a godly person. I'm sure they only became "confused" by my incongruent actions and words. I have prayed many times for God to make my crooked paths straight. *"For God is not the author of confusion but of peace, as in all the churches of the saints"* (1 Cor. 14:33).

C. This stage of "confusion" creates a need for acceptance from those around us. We want to be loved, accepted and seen as part of the crowd. This is part of the fallen nature of *every* man. Due to this, we tend to listen to conversations we should not, and to say things that are detrimental to us and those around us. James 3:6 tells us, *"And the tongue is a fire, a world of iniquity. The tongue is so set among our members that it defiles the whole body..."* All around us are examples of people speaking gossip, slander and giving evil reports about their spouses, friends, supervisors and neighbors. No wonder we get so confused by these negative comments! We must be wary of conversations which appear to lean toward mocking and putting people down. Think back to the last time you heard something negative about a person. Who shared it with you? Most likely, it was told to you by someone considered close in relationship. As we become more immersed in the layers of confusion, our filtering process (discernment) begins to minimize. Soon we are listening to conversations that weeks before we would have walked away from due to their content.

God has asked us to mature in our Christian walks. We must move from "spiritual milk" to "solid food." It is my contention that to discern good from evil is one way to move into the solid food to which Christ refers to in the Book of Hebrews. We must begin to walk and act maturely, separating ourselves from evil ways and recognizing those who are the messengers of evil. *"But solid food belongs to those who are of full age (mature), that is, those who by reason of use have their senses exercised to discern both good and evil"* (Hebrews 5:14). Shake off this level of confusion, see and understand who are the people who tend to defile others by their conversation. These are not the people we need to "hang around." Being accepted by them is not something to brag about in your prayer time. "Oh Lord, thank you that I am not like that person over there, who is without a multitude of friends." This type of prayer was used by the Pharisees which only led them to a spiritual death.

There are those of us who have a strong "mercy" tendency. Many Christians believe that mercy means that we don't confront people. Challenging someone may hurt his or her feelings and we worry about being rude. I can hear it now; "But Mike, if I stop a person from saying something or if I refuse to listen, isn't that rude?" I'll tell you what is rude. It is rude to knowingly be a part of gossip. It is not "good manners" to listen to verbal assaults and the blatant character assassinations of people who are not even present to defend themselves. It is foolishness and ignorance. We must open our eyes and discern who is giving the evil reports.

D. We can be **"confused" as to what are the true intentions of an individual and what motivates their false report.** The following ten areas are not meant to be an exhaustive list. There are other motivations that create a heart of impurity and encourage evil reports. If you think of others, add them to this list and investigate ways to prevent them from impacting your life. This list should, however, give the reader some insight and understanding why an individual would use the weapon of an evil report to attack another person.

Underlying Motivations for Giving an Evil Report

1. ANGER—The emotions of anger are fueled by many different situations. Once we allow anger to consume us, all else seems insignificant. Relationships, appearances, what others think or say, all become minuscule compared to the explosion of anger. What can be termed as "rage" overcomes a person and they no longer think logically. When this occurs, that person is in the affective realm (emotional state) and not in the cognitive realm (thinking state). It is common to say

and do things that we are later remorseful for and wish we had not done. (Do I hear an amen?) Our emotions take over and we become defensive. *"Let all bitterness, wrath, **anger**, clamor and evil speaking be put away from you, with all malice"* (Eph. 4:31) (emphasis added).

2. BITTERNESS—When we react, due to personal hurts and rejection, the area of bitterness is involved (see Eph. 4:31 above). *"For I see you are poisoned by **bitterness**..."* (Acts 8:23) (emphasis added). Bitterness can easily lead to a sense of wanting revenge against a person. "I want to get back at them for what they did," or "I'll get even," become common phrases in the minds of bitter people. There is a statement people may use in jest: "I don't get mad, I get even." This is the motto of the bitter person.

3. MOCKING—Evil reports may be motivated by a spirit of mockery, making fun of others or putting people down. *"Do not be deceived, God is not **mocked**; for whatever a man sows that he will also reap"* (Gal. 6:7) (emphasis added). When we mock another person, we are causing injury or pain to one of God's creations. It is as if we are mocking God and the way he fashioned His creation. The mocking spirit was found in the Pharisees, in the enemies of Israel and in the world today by those who oppose the gospel of Jesus Christ. Be careful, if we sow mocking into the world, into relationships, the Bible says that same spirit will be reaped by each one of us.

4. DECEIT—It becomes commonplace for deceitful people to believe that giving an evil report is okay. This person convinces himself that the other person deserves whatever fate befalls them, and it is okay to help "fate" along with its direction. *"For from within,*

out of the heart of men, proceed evil thoughts...wickedness, deceit..." (Mark 7:21, 22) (emphasis added). Deceit is like a blinder—the kind that horses may need to wear to keep their focus forward, or in one direction. When we are deceived, we can only see one way—OUR WAY. This leads to misunderstandings, stubbornness and a refusal to learn and to be teachable.

5. ENVY—Our jealousy and envy may come from desiring what other people have in their lives. God has blessed each one of us. If you are feeling shortchanged, ask the Lord to reveal to you those "precious gems" which you don't see in your life. It is not uncommon to find that others are feeling envious of a gift or a talent that we have. How odd that we spend so much time and energy coveting what is not ours and so little time and energy cultivating that which is given to us by God. We don't need what others have, we need to appreciate what God has given us. *"A sound heart is life to the body, but **envy** is rottenness to the bones"* (Prov. 14:30) (emphasis added). Don't covet! Cultivate!

6. SELF-SEEKING—When **our** priorities, **our** desires, **our** wants and **our** ambitions become more important than seeking God's direction in our life, we become self-absorbed and self-seeking. I honestly know that there have been times when I have placed God on the throne of my life. I also know, there are times I have taken Him off the throne. I don't want *my* mind and soul to make decisions. Inevitably, those decisions don't prove to be fruitful. When *my will* prevails, I (we) never know how it will turn out. *"For where envy and **self-seeking** exist, confusion and every evil thing are*

there" (Jas. 3:16) (emphasis added).

7. GUILT—When we attempt to justify our past actions, mistakes and attitudes, we can be motivated by guilt. It is apparent that we have made an error, but we are unwilling to admit the mistake, so we cover it up by slandering another person. Instead, we should recognize that we all make mistakes, we all are sinners, but are saved by grace. *"For whoever shall keep the whole law, and yet stumble in one point, he is **guilty** of all"* (Jas. 2:10) (emphasis added). We *will* make mistakes. Our struggle begins when we attempt to be "perfect" and not learn from our mistakes. Imagine that I am baking a cake (Now don't be sexist. I am a good cook.) being perfect in measuring out every ingredient, so precisely calculating along the way. During this process, I leave out the baking powder, or I bake it too long. (Okay, so maybe I'm not that good a cook.) No matter how perfect I am with the rest of the cake-baking process, the entire cake is ruined. The only recourse is to start over. In life, we must ask for forgiveness and begin to rebuild the relationship again.

8. OFFENSES—Being offended at one another, holding in hurts and bitterness will lead to speaking evil of another person. Truly, if we become upset with another and "offended," it becomes our sin. God has commanded us to love our neighbors, love our enemies, to submit one to another. There is no place to become offended at one another. Offenses separate us from God. We have been given a complete and clear process in Matthew 18 on how we are to respond when offenses come to our lives. *"Woe to the world because of **offenses**! For offenses must come, but woe to that man by whom the offense comes"* (Matt. 18:7) (emphasis added).

9. REBELLION—It becomes possible for us to justify an "independent" spirit by slipping into rebellion. When we realize that we have violated the Holy Spirit and His intent for our lives, we can either repent or rebel. Unfortunately, there are those of us who choose rebellion. *"For **rebellion** is as the sin of witchcraft, and stubbornness is as iniquity and idolatry"* (1 Sam. 15:23) (emphasis added). Jezebel is an excellent (or rather, I should say, poor) example of one who felt justified to operate outside of the realm of God's will. In 1 Kings, chapter 18, we read of Jezebel's cutting off and killing the prophets of the Lord. The envious, jealous and ungodly nature of Jezebel is revealed in 1 Kings 21. Naboth owned a vineyard next to the palace of King Ahab. The king asked to buy or trade vineyards with Naboth, as it would have been convenient for the king to own the vineyard next to his palace. Naboth respectfully declined as the vineyard was an inheritance and had sentimental value.

When King Ahab's wife, Jezebel, heard about this, she was undaunted. She simply set up false accusations against Naboth and had him killed. According to people in rebellion, laws, rules and guidelines are for other individuals. Rebels violate people verbally, physically and emotionally. Be careful! Rebellion is a sinister companion and can turn a "kind, gentle spirit" into one that is "cruel and insensitive."

10. PRIDE—We want to exalt ourselves instead of serving and preferring others. This is commonly demonstrated by putting others down in order to build ourselves up. *"**Pride** goes before destruction, and a haughty spirit before a fall"* (Proverbs 16:18) (emphasis added). When we operate in pride, we might as well tell Jesus to

"move off the throne" of our lives. Who is in charge of your life? I grieve every time I become aware of my prideful nature which places Jesus back up on the cross. Our Lord died for our sins, but He was resurrected and sits at the right hand of the Father. The Holy Spirit embodies each and every believer who will receive Him.

Jesus Christ is **not** on the cross. The Holy Spirit is not just "Blowin' in the Wind." He abides within us. However, each time I sin and allow my soulish pride to overwhelm my godly spirit, it is as if Jesus is back on the cross, dying and shedding His blood for me. I want my prayer to be, "Lord, please be on the throne of my life. I willingly give up my position and exalt You as King and ruler over me." Will you join with me in this prayer?

If we can begin to grasp the foundational motivations of people who speak evil, we can prevent our lives from being defiled by listening to the evil report. Yes, it does take self-control; it does take a willingness to be accountable to others; it does require each one of us to seek God for our own personal areas of sin. However, as we press into the presence of God, He faithfully exposes weaknesses in our armor. And just as faithfully, He supplies new armor.

E. A person may become **"confused" as to how detrimental it is to listen to gossip, murmuring, etc...**That is, we find that we enjoy hearing gossip because it exalts us. Gossip tears down those we may dislike, whom we are jealous or envious of, or people whom we desire to see hurt, because they may have hurt us.

> *The time is coming when people won't listen to good teaching. Instead they will look for teachers who will please them by telling them only what they are itching to hear. They will turn from the truth and eager-*

ly listen to senseless stories.
2 Timothy 4:3, 4, CEV

Those who are drawn to gossip and slander have set themselves toward listening to "senseless and foolish" stories.

The more we listen to slander and tale bearing, the more we become callous as to their impact on our lives. This is the same for many other areas of life. If we watch violent movies and fill our thoughts with pornography and lust, we become desensitized to the sin. Our parameters and boundaries become stretched. One beer becomes two, then three, then a six-pack a night. A movie with some questionable content allows us to rationalize watching a movie with explicit sexual content. The more we expose ourselves to negative comments, sinful speech and acts of character defamation, the more likely we will be to become actively involved in these same areas. **The nature of sin always takes you farther than you want to go; costs more than you want to pay; and it keeps you longer than you want to stay.** It is a road we shouldn't go down, for once we do, it is easy to get lost, and it takes a long time to get home.

F. One becomes **"confused" as to how Satan uses evil reports**. What may seem as an innocent discussion among friends, may be used by the enemy to create multiple problems in the kingdom of God.

> *For we do not wrestle against flesh and blood, but against principalities, against powers, against the rulers of the darkness of this age, against spiritual hosts of wickedness in the heavenly places.*
> *Eph. 6:12*

Our involvement in ungodly conversation will impact every area of our lives. It is impossible to isolate the cancer of sin from infecting our entire "body." There are five main areas that seem to be regularly "attacked" when people are involved in gossip, talebearing and murmuring—you know, evil reports.

How Satan Uses "Evil Reports"

1. Satan will use an evil report to destroy families. Satan can, and will, gain an advantage over each one of us if we are confused and ignorant to his ways. We must be aware of the destructive powers involved in listening to a distorted, untrue, or evil word. When people follow a path

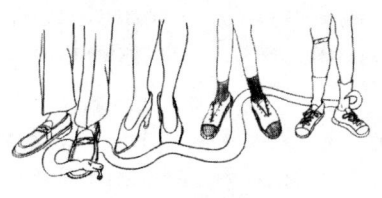

of confusion, it allows them to fall prey to many deceptive situations. Through confusion, many people are taken advantage of financially, physically and emotionally.

Confusion should not be an excuse for our failures. The Bible is very clear in speaking to us about evil reports. It also commands us to be wise and not have our head in the sand regarding Satan's evil ways, "...*lest Satan should take advantage of us; for we are not ignorant of his devices*"(2 Cor. 2:11). One of his devices is clearly the use of confusion in our lives. Through prayer, accountability and reading the Word of God, keep your mind clear and focused on the truth of God.

2. Satan uses evil reports to attack spiritual leadership and undermine their authority in the Church and the "Kingdom of God." An unsupportive comment such as, "Can you believe how strongly the pastor spoke about marriage? It isn't as if he doesn't have his own problems," becomes misconstrued which now becomes a weapon of Satan to bludgeon the pastor and his family. "I heard the pastor is having marriage problems" begins to filter through the congregation.

Listen carefully at how often negative reports are directed at leadership—not just spiritual leaders—but leaders in general. Seldom is there an attack against the person who lacks vision, or who is without direction. However, put purpose in someone's heart, let him speak of destiny and a calling on his life and suddenly, attacks abound. The enemy does not want your spiritual leaders to have your support, prayers, or encouragement. Moses found this to be true with the children of Israel. Throughout the book of Exodus, Moses is undermined by the people. They came against his decisions, his direction and questioned whether he truly heard from God. This cycle is one which seems to permeate the "Church" at large.

3. Satan may use a false report to create an atmosphere that separates brother from brother, and sister from sister. In 2 Samuel, we find the story of Mephibosheth, the son of Jonathan. King David wanted to honor those who were in the house of Saul, any offspring of Jonathan, as a way of continuing his covenant to the former king (2 Sam 9). The servant of Jonathan, Ziba, was jealous and attempted to separate the heart of David from Mephibosheth (2 Samuel 16:1-4). Because of Ziba's lies and deception, King David thought Mephibosheth was out to reclaim the kingdom and overthrow David. Nothing was ever substantiated. David was only responding to what Ziba had stated, which was an evil report. He then took away all that was given to Mephibosheth and gave it to Ziba. In 2 Samuel, we find David and Mephibosheth confronting one another.

> *"...the king said, "Why did you not go with me, Mephibosheth?" And he answered, "My lord, o king, my servant deceived me. For your servant said, 'I will saddle a donkey for myself, that I may ride on it*

and go to the king,' because your servant is lame. And Ziba slandered your servant to my lord the king..."

                                                         2 Sam. 19:24-27

Once David realized that he had listened to an evil report, he corrected his error by blessing Mephibosheth with the land that David had formerly taken. Satan's desire is to separate God's people from one another and to create a barrier between the people and their God-given leaders.

4. Satan desires to divide and conquer. The Bible tells us that God is not the author of confusion (1 Cor. 14:33). If it isn't God, then it must be Satan, Lucifer, Slewfoot, the guy with the pitchfork and the red suit. Come on people, wake up!! There is an enemy and his job is to "steal, kill and destroy" (John 10:10). Satan is out to "seek whom he may devour" (1 Pet. 5:8). Satan and all his demonic forces do not want unity among Christians; they do not want unity among churches; they certainly do not want peace to reign in our lives. Each and every evil report will be twisted and turned to the benefit of God's enemies. What side of the fence do you fall on?

5. Satan uses evil reports to degrade the name of Jesus Christ. How many newspaper headlines have decried the work of a godly person? *"Right Wing Religious Fanatics," "Ultra Conservative Legalistic Christians," "Narrow Minded Zealots"* are just a few of the headlines depicting God's people. I understand that there are people who have sinned and must be held accountable for their inappropriate and ungodly actions. However, the way some are vilified and castigated, often within the Christian community, is contrary to God's way. The Body of Christ (the Church at large) should be a testimony of prayer, of compassion and of restoration. When a brother or sister falls into a sinful pattern, our greatest desire should be for restoration not consequences, for repentance not persecution, for humility not embarrassment. What are **we** modeling to the unbeliever? Our approach and response to sin and failure should be a source of encouragement and strength to unbelievers. They need to see that "We don't shoot our wounded." but we pray for God's healing in their lives. This will help those who are far from God to willingly draw near Him, without fear of reprisal from within the Christian sector.

As we conclude this section, if there is an area in which God has convicted your heart, take time and repent. Allow God to cleanse your heart, purify your spirit from defilement and to guide your tongue in future conversations. We can have our habit patterns changed by an intervention from the Holy Spirit. We are not bound by our past mistakes. Jesus Christ brings freedom to the captives. We must make our primary desire to seek His kingdom and His righteousness. Once again, willingly place God on the throne of your life.

QUESTIONS— Examining the Heart

1. When you are "confused," how do you respond to people around you? Do you attack people? Do you become defensive? Overly critical? Overly sensitive?

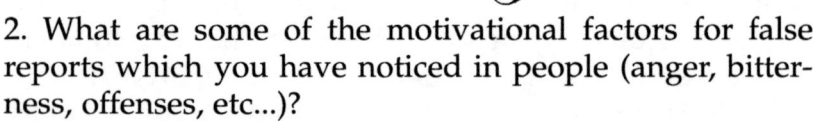

2. What are some of the motivational factors for false reports which you have noticed in people (anger, bitterness, offenses, etc...)?

3. In your personal life, what can you do to prevent becoming bound by confusion?

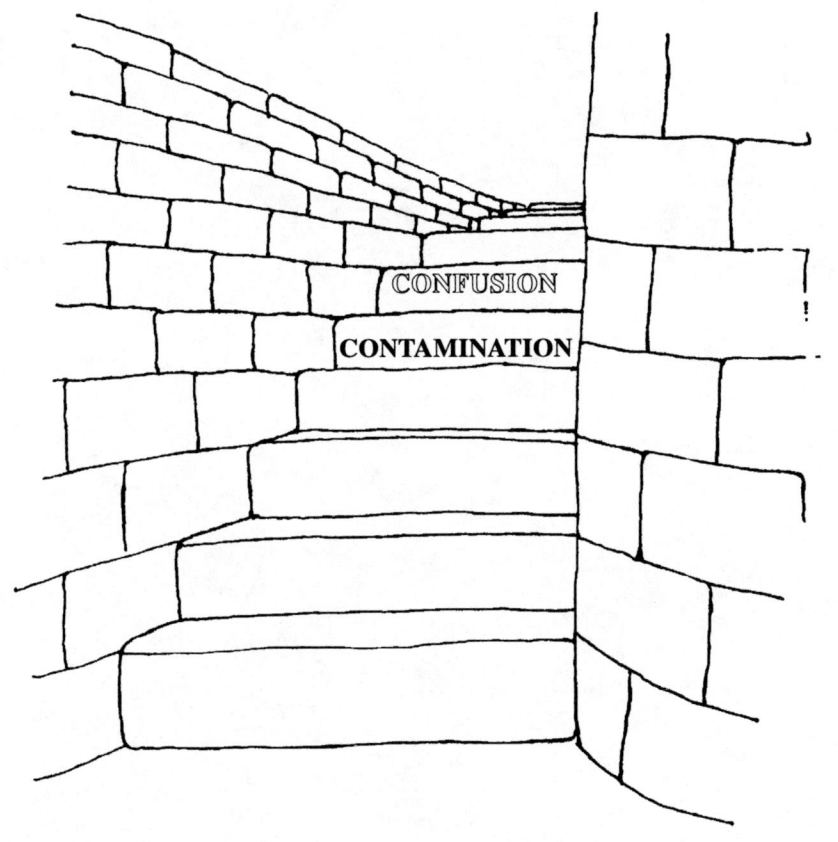

CHAPTER 5

CONTAMINATION

Prior to entering the full-time pastoral ministry, I worked for fifteen years in the public school setting. My role in the schools included being a social worker/counselor for many years and then, for my final six years, I worked as a classroom teacher. It was during my time as an educator that I experienced (and participated) in a saturation of evil reports. The teacher's lounge is a dangerous place, if one is wanting to avoid negative discussions. Don't misunderstand what I am saying or misinterpret my illustration. I am not suggesting that all schools are a haven for evil reports, though many would probably qualify for an "A" in Rumor Mill 101. I am stating that the "world" is a conglomeration of people, many of whom are in active sin, and who lack understanding and teachings as to the danger of gossip and the spreading of rumors. This is true for many businesses in both the private and public sectors. Since the bulk of my personal experiences were grounded in the public school setting, my illustrations naturally follow that experience.

Behind Closed Doors

The teachers' lounge is a place for educators to sit and talk without a student or parent being present. Most schools have a "No Admittance" policy for students, or, certainly have them knock on the lounge door and wait outside for a response. This carefully constructed off-limits sector provides the opportunity for educators to talk about people, without fear of their discussions being overheard. It was not uncommon to have an educator speak negatively about a student or parent only to have another educator chime in with similar frustrations. As the feeding frenzy continued, this unsuspecting student or parent was "filleted" unmercifully by the educators. It seemed that as these discussions continued, the educators became more and more bitter toward the student or parent. Their anger increased and soon, a rationale for revenge, punishment or retreating emotionally became the foundation for the relationship between the people. *"As surely as rain blows in from the north, anger is caused by cruel words"* (Prov. 25:23, CEV).

- Were the comments accurate?
- Did the educators involved share situations which actually occurred?
- Isn't it okay to just vent and receive moral support?

Whether the comments or situations shared were an accurate reflection of the student is not the issue. The Bible states that gossip and cruel words only create more strife. If a person is sharing their frustration in order to receive counsel for future interactions, we have a different scenario. Most situations reveal stories and gossip being used to elicit support and sympathy for the gossip, **not to cover and aid the victim**. The "attempt" at restoration is seldom seen within the confines of the world.

A teachers' lounge is not the only place where people speak negatively of others. At your workplace, there may be a staff lounge, a lunchroom or a designated area where people gather or meet each day. At a school, it might be the cafeteria, the playground or the front of the school.

In a church, during choir rehearsals or board meetings, the temptation to murmur is constantly before us. In a home, one might use the living or family room to entertain people (with gossip). We certainly use the telephone as a channel for our negative expressions toward others. Identify the places where gossip and rumors begin to prevail in your life. Set up an action plan to avoid or minimize your involvement in these areas. Share this plan with another and hold yourself accountable. Minimizing gossip will definitely decrease the anger and frustration in the lives of people who are normally "touched" by this type of conversation.

> *Where there is no fuel a fire goes out; where there is not gossip arguments come to an end. Troublemakers start trouble, just as sparks and fuel start a fire.*
> Prov. 26:20, 21, CEV

We can change habit patterns and therefore help change the patterns of those we come in contact with each day. Remember, only YOU can prevent forest fires. (Note the aforementioned Proverb.)

Negative Conversations

What if you are in situations that do not allow you to leave or to change physical location? Do we always need to confront people? Isn't there a time to just be quiet and not say anything? Let me give two examples which I think would best answer these questions. The first example will help an individual learn how to minimize, or even shut down, a negative discussion in a large group setting. I did not always have the freedom, nor did I desire, to always leave the room where the gossip was occurring. However, I became aware of the impact it was having on my spirit and my attitude. One approach which I found effective when wanting to negate the gossip in a discussion was to join in on the conversation. (What? Join in on the negative, damaging discussions? Stay with me for a few more sentences.) One thing you will notice is that these discussions are open to anybody, especially those who fuel the fire. My comments were intended to *throw water on the fire,* **not gasoline**. One person might say, "Jimmy is such a frustration. He never gets his work done and he is so lazy." (As you can see, this statement has no merit toward restoration for Jimmy. It is only meant to gain sympathy or support for the person speaking the assertions.) My response might be "I also have Jimmy in class. Have you noticed the last week or so his work is really improving?"

If the person answers with a negative or flippant response, "No, I think he is getting worse."

I, again, respond with a positive, "Maybe he does better for me because I have him in the morning." or "He is doing better for me, hopefully it will carry over."

Imagine you are at a friend's house and the person begins to speak negatively about their spouse. This is, unfortunately, very common, as you well know. "My husband/wife is driving me crazy. He/she is so inconsiderate and selfish sometimes. I can hardly stand to be around him/her."

While this comment is born out of hurt and frustration, it can be the beginning of a complaining and grumbling spirit. Instead of asking the person to give you more details, there might be a more effective response to minimize the damage of an evil report. "It sounds as if you are really hurting. Have you talked with the pastor or a leader to receive counsel?" After their response, you may reply, "I am going to commit to pray each day for your marriage. I know God has a destiny and plan for both of you. Satan would love to destroy what God has intentioned for you, but I want to join with you to prevent further damage. In fact, let's pray now."

If the person is a non-Christian, you can still respond in a way that circumvents further negative discussion. "It sounds as if you are really hurting. Marriage really takes a lot of work and can be a bit overwhelming at times. I'm sure if you need some guidance, there are good counselors available. For me, I usually talk with my pastor and devote myself to prayer. I will begin to pray more for your marriage, as well."

These types of positive approaches shut down the tendency for others to add additional negative comments. It is a funny (or perhaps sad) thing about evil reports, our carnal nature desires to touch them and to entertain them. Unfortunately, we are not always repulsed by these conversations. In fact, many times, we are lured into them by the enticing aroma and taste of sin. It is true that many of us like to be in the midst of conversations and "in the know" in discussions, but the remnant of such discussions is often sorrow and pain. *"The words of a talebearer are as wounds, and they go down into the innermost parts of the belly"* (Prov. 18:8, KJV).

I realize that the above example and illustration encourages an individual to boldly speak against the murmuring and gossip in a conversation. This is not easy to do and can make for awkward moments. There are some of us who don't feel comfortable confronting situations and hope, and pray, those situations will simply disappear. "If I just don't say anything, they will get the idea I am not a part of their discussion and not interested in their opinions" is often their reasoning.

Have there ever been times where I, personally, didn't say anything, which therefore allowed someone to speak inappropriately of another? Yes, unfortunately, many times. I am a man-pleaser at times. I fear the responses of certain people. There were times when I should have left the room, made a contrary statement (a positive comment) or asked for further clarification. My unwillingness to intervene was due to my carnal nature. This is not an excuse, but simply a confession of my inadequacies and my lack of strength in certain situations. I need God to make me bolder in those scenarios and to give me wisdom as to how to interact in difficult situations. The Bible **never** encourages us to sit by, in the midst of sin, and hope it goes away. As Christians, we are called to be light in a dark world, not to be consumed by darkness.

Words of Truth

- *"Flee sexual immorality..."* (1 Cor. 6:18).
- *"Therefore, my beloved, flee from idolatry"* (1 Cor. 10:14).
- *"Let your light so shine before men..."* (Matt. 5:16).
- *"Flee also youthful lusts..."* (2 Tim. 2:22).
- *"For you were once darkness, but now you are light in the Lord. Walk as children of light"* (Eph. 5:8).

In speaking of Babylon, a representation of an evil, decadent society, Jeremiah writes, *"Flee from the midst of Babylon, and everyone save his life!"* (Jer. 51:6). We find a strong word and direction in Proverbs 13:19, *"A desire accomplished is sweet to the soul, but it is an abomination to fools to depart from evil."* The Contemporary English Version says this in a little stronger way, *"It's a good feeling to get what you want, but only a stupid fool hates to turn from evil."* We are called to be a light to the world and are commanded to flee from evil, to turn our backs on the ungodly ways of gossip, murmuring, talebearing, whispering, any area which leads us into listening to an evil report.

For my second example, let me explain why there needs to be a response, either verbally or physically (i.e. leaving the area). I recently received a phone call from a telephone solicitor. Naturally, the call came at a most inconvenient time (Is there ever a convenient time for these calls?). The individual on the phone began with the usual greetings, "How are you tonight, Mr. Sedler?"

Inwardly, I knew where this might be heading, but, as usual, I responded with a chatty, "Fine, thank you."

The voice went on to say, "Would you like to improve the quality of your relationship with your wife?" This was a loaded question. If I said, "No," it might appear as though I don't care about my wife. What if Joyce is testing me? Did she ask someone to find out my innermost feelings? Perhaps it was someone from church who had been through our marriage classes and was seeing if I really "walk the walk." Oh! The pressure was mounting. In a moment of weakness and foolishness, I responded as many people would, "I have a good relationship with my wife, but of course, it could be better." That was all the person needed to continue his forthcoming "persuasive speech." For the next several minutes, they told me about a magazine that would supposedly enhance every facet of our relationship. I waited for them to take a breath so I could respond, but they must have had on an oxygen tank! I casually listened, with the opportunity for only an occasional "Yes...uh-huh...," and a few nods of the head (as if that were discernible over the phone.) As the salesperson wound down their monologue, and I was ready to interject, "No thank you," they took a turn which caused me to stutter and stumble verbally.

The person concluded their sales pitch with the comment, "Now, Mr. Sedler, do you have a credit card?"

I replied with a terse, "Yes."

The salesperson stated, "Well, Mr. Sedler, we can bill you and have you pay $29.99 by check for a one year subscription or you can use your credit card and pay $24.99 for one year. Which would you like?" This was not going as I planned. My response of "no, thank you" did not fit into the options I was given. After several awkward minutes and gentle combat, I hung up the phone. I was frustrated at the time I had wasted on the phone, but even more uptight over what I felt was the audacity of the sales person to assume I wanted their magazine. Did I want to use a check or credit card? Really!! (I naturally chose the credit card to save the $5.00.)

I was recently talking with a friend and, during the course of our conversation, he explained a term that helped me understand the approach of the magazine solicitor. It also helped me to see the importance of responding and not just sitting silently during an ungodly situation. (I am not suggesting the magazine situation was ungodly, I am referring to ungodly conversations.) My friend explained that in the business realm, there is a term called *Implied Consent*. Many salespeople use this as a ploy to get customers to buy their merchandise. The tone of the conversation, from the salesperson, is always focused on the sale of the merchandise. It is assumed that the person will buy the product and all discussion is geared toward making the sale as compatible for the consumer as possible. My silence was only allowing the salesperson to "weave a large web" around me. In business terms, my silence was implying that I consented to buy the product. If you are in the sales field, do not be alarmed by my analogy. The person who called did nothing wrong. They were polite, but persuasive. If I had responded in a disinterested fashion sooner, the conversation would have ended more quickly. This is true for carriers of evil reports. The sooner I respond in a contrary way, the quicker the conversation will end. Are you involved in "implied consent" with those who are sharing an evil report?

In the previous chapters, I discussed what an evil report is, how we can prepare ourselves to recognize a false report and the initial stairstep leading to defilement — "Confusion." In future chapters, there will be an exploration into the impact of an "evil report" upon our spirits. If we are unaware of the power of an "evil report," that same power can destroy friendships, make us unclean spiritually, allow us to be more susceptible to other evil reports or even place us in a position to become an unwitting pawn of Satan. The enemy desires to discredit people in leadership positions, to break kindred Christian bonds with a brother or sister, and certainly to present us as poor witnesses to non-Christians regarding our Christian attitudes.

The second stage (or stairstep) which can occur by hearing a negative report will be called **"contamination."** This occurs when we willingly listen to negative talk. We may know what is happening, but we refuse to stop it.

CONTAMINATION: Exposing one's spirit to uncleanness and ungodliness through sinful conversations.

The stages being presented are hierarchical in nature. If we are in a state of **"confusion"** as to what is occurring, we will have a tendency to become involved in the conversation, which leads to the **"contamination"** of our spirit. Each stairstep will slowly and methodically lead us into the depths of defilement. Hopefully, as you read this book, you will find biblical and practical ways to avoid the snare of the enemy.

Imagine we are in a factory, wandering around and investigating the contents of the work area. There is a large sign on the door.

"Do Not Enter—Contamination"

It is safe to assume that we would not enter that room knowing that it is almost certainly a danger to our lives. What if there were no sign? What if, during our inspection, we found ourselves in the midst of a contaminated room, exposed to the dangers associated with radioactive materials? We would certainly flee the area and get medical attention.

The next time we went to that same factory, the interior of the contaminated room would not be part of our tour, right? Then why do we continue to place ourselves in situations where we constantly become contaminated by unhealthy and ungodly language, discussions and conversations? The pollution from these conversations are every bit as deadly as that of radioactive materials. Our lives will be filled with pain and suffering, creating a tremendous impact on those around us.

This is an important issue to God. His Word consistently and repeatedly draws our attention to it. He clearly tells us what will happen to those involved in spreading "evil reports." *"Whoever secretly **slanders** his neighbor, him I will destroy; The one who has a haughty and proud heart, him I will not endure"* (Psa. 101:5) (emphasis added). Another translation says, *"Anyone who spreads **gossip** will be silenced, and no one who is conceited will be my friend"* (CEV) (emphasis added). What is God referring to when He says, *"a haughty and proud heart, him I will not endure"* or *"no one conceited will be my friend?"* I see a person with a "proud heart" or an individual with blatant "conceit" as one who feels they can do what they desire, even if it is outside the realm of God. This person's arrogance allows them to believe they are above God's laws and, supposedly, will receive no repercussions for their sin. Perhaps, this would be a person who believes they can associate with carriers of evil reports, surround themselves with ungodly conversations, subject themselves to crude discussions, and emerge unscathed. After all, "I can handle it," "It won't affect me," or even, "I'm strong enough to resist," have all been said by those who, eventually, are drawn into total "contamination and exposure" in their spirits. How about you? Have you said or thought these phrases, believing that you would be exempt from "contamination?"

There are times we recognize that the conversation is heading toward an ungodly discussion. There are also times when we follow the suggested approaches found in previous chapters, asking questions in an attempt to understand and clarify the motivation of those involved in the discussion. We may ask the following questions: "Do you need to be telling me this information?" "Where did you get your information?" "Have you talked directly with the people involved in this scenario?" "Hey scumbag, is this an evil report?" (Just testing you to be sure you weren't skipping over this review material. I know, I know, it is just like a teacher to always be reviewing and testing people.) So, what happens after you have questioned the person and made it clear that you are not interested in being a part of their "evil report," but they persist in telling you? At this point, we **must** take a stand.

This may seem harsh or strong to some people, but the *magnitude of the consequences* for not taking a stand **far exceeds** any discomfort or concerns about hurting the speaker's feelings. The Book of Ephesians explains clearly what our response should be when confronted with *"foolish talking or course jesting"* (5:4). Let me share a few verses in Ephesians 5:8-12:

> *For you were once darkness, but now you are light in the Lord. Walk as children of light (for the fruit of the Spirit is in all goodness, righteousness, and truth), finding out what is acceptable to the Lord. And have no fellowship with the unfruitful works of darkness, but rather expose them. For it is shameful even to speak of those things which are done by them in secret.*

Another reference as to how we should respond to the carriers of evil reports is found in Romans 16:17, *"Now I urge you, brethren, note those who cause divisions and offenses, contrary to the doctrine which you learned, and avoid them."* I do not want to belabor the point, but I do desire for us to see the importance God has placed on avoiding people who create strife, division and speak evil of others.

Natural and Spiritual Senses

Contamination must be avoided or we set ourselves in a position to contaminate other people. Physically, we have been equipped with warning systems to prevent contamination by our surroundings. We can tell if the air around us is foul, has dangerous contaminates, by our *sense of smell*. We are able to visually detect if the surroundings appear hazardous by our *sense of sight*. It is our *sense of touch* which gives us a warning if something is too hot or too sharp and may cause damage to our body. *Our sense of taste* warns us if food is rancid or milk is sour. Finally, we become aware of loud, dangerous noises which are pollution to us by our *sense of hearing*. These are five physical ways which we can identify contamination around us. They are warning systems to protect us from potentially dangerous and defiling circumstances.

In the same way, God has provided us with protective spiritual defenses which warn us of spiritual contamination. These spiritual defenses may utilize our five physical senses to enhance their perception, but the spiritual defenses operate in a realm independent of the physical senses. Listed below are a few examples of these spiritual defenses which God has made available to us.

1. **Discernment**—Through the gift of the Holy Spirit (1 Cor. 12:10) we have the ability to:

- *"discern between good and evil"* (2 Sam. 14:17; 1 Kings

3:9; Heb. 5:14).

- *"discern the thoughts and intents of the heart"* (Heb. 4:12).
- *"discern between the righteous and the wicked"* (Mal. 3:18).

2. **Wisdom**—Through the gift of the Holy Spirit (1 Cor. 12:8) we are able to:

- *"receive wisdom from God"* (Prov. 2:6; James 1:5).
- *"receive a pure, peaceable wisdom with good fruits and without hypocrisy"* (James 3:17).
- *"receive wisdom, a more precious gift than gold"* (Prov. 16:16).

3. **Knowledge**—Through the gift of the Holy Spirit (1 Cor. 12:8) we are able to:

- *"see things in the spirit, not seen in the flesh"* (Jer. 11:18).
- *"abound in knowledge as well as abound in the grace of God"* (2 Cor. 8:7).
- *"show our knowledge by our good conduct and conversation"* (James 3:13).

4. **Revelation**—Through the gift of the Holy Spirit (Eph. 1:17) we are able to:

- *"bring a profitable word to those around us"* (1 Cor. 14:6).
- *"receive understanding beyond the natural"* (Gal. 1:12).

We can, and need to, sensitize ourselves to the prompting of the Holy Spirit. We must follow God's word and obey the wise counsel of those in leadership and pastoral authority over us. God has placed a governmental hierarchy throughout His kingdom including our personal lives, our marriages, our families, the church. These "checks and balances" are available for our protection spiritually. The Bible tells us about *"submitting to one another"* in Ephesians 5:21, *"submitting to elders in the church"* in 1 Peter 5:5 and of finding *"safety in the multitude of counselors"* in Proverbs 11:14. If we use the resources God has given us—prayer, the Word of God, the fellowship of believers, we can recognize the defilement of conversation before it impacts us. Be aware of your physical and spiritual defenses and contamination will be minimized. We have been given the authority to battle, and be victorious, over the wiles of Satan. *"I give you the authority...over all the power of the enemy, and nothing shall by any means hurt you"* (Luke 10:19). My friends, be confident of the authority, power and anointing in which God allows us to operate in when we are joined with His Spirit.

QUESTIONS—Examining the Heart

1. Have you been contaminated within this past week?

2. Is there anyone you can think of who regularly contaminates you with their speech patterns?

3. Can you think of a time when you took a stand and refused to be a part of the contaminating conversation?

CHAPTER 6

FOOLISHNESS

The third stairstep or stage that may occur when listening to an evil report is called **"foolishness."**

FOOLISHNESS: Allowing an evil report to influence your thinking and discernment about people and situations.

As the conversation unfolds and a person is presented in a negative light, the ensuing emotions often lead us to take up an offense toward the person being discussed in the evil report. "Confusion" and "contamination" have softened our defenses and we fall into the trap of being sympathetic to the charges against a person. Our lack of discernment and wisdom can lead us to believe the accusations against an individual without ever checking out the facts or hearing, as Paul Harvey says, "the rest of the story."

Over the years, I have had many people ask me to help them identify these "carriers of evil reports." You may wonder if there is a way to categorize them. Is it possible to put "people of defilement" into specific categories and thereby identify them more quickly in life? These are excellent questions that have motivated me to focus on seven examples of people who give evil reports. The Bible speaks about each of these people, their character and the impact of their actions. This is not an attempt to categorize people to label them or place them into a "box" of condemnation. This list is not exhaustive and is to be used only as a guideline for further revelation from God. The following examples are intended to help identify an evil report quickly and to avoid being defiled by ungodly conversation.

Seven Types of Evil Reporters

1. The Backbiter—*One who speaks against an absent individual.*

The backbiter, to be sure, does not follow a Matthew 18 principle. All accusations and comments are made without the accused being present. Psalm 15:2,3 speaks of this type of individual. David inquires of God as to who will dwell in His presence. *"He who walks uprightly and works righteousness and speaks the truth in his heart; He who does not backbite with his tongue, nor does evil to his neighbor, nor does he take up a reproach against his friend."* The word used for *backbiters* in Romans 1:30 is the word *katalalos* (Strong's

Exhaustive Concordance #2637) which means "talkative against." Let me quote Romans 1:28-30 so you may get the full impact of this word:

*And even as they did not like to retain God in their knowledge, God gave them over to a debased mind, to do those things which are not fitting; being filled with all unrighteousness, sexual immorality, wickedness, covetousness, maliciousness; full of envy, murder, strife, deceit, evil-mindedness; they are whisperers, **backbiters**, haters of God, violent, proud, boasters, inventors of evil things, disobedient to parents...* (emphasis added)

God places backbiting in the same company as the haters of God as well as other ungodly activities and actions. God is telling His people to avoid these situations (see also Prov. 25:23; 2 Cor. 12:20).

2. **The Busybody—***One who seeks out information on a false report and spreads it by means of gossip, slander, backbiting, etc.*

God considers this to be very serious. He sees this as deadly as many other sins. In fact, God categorizes being a busybody with that of being an evildoer or even a killer. Now, I know some of you think this is mere sensationalism or exaggeration. I have it on good authority (the Bible) that this is true. *"But let none of you suffer as a murderer, a thief, an evildoer, or as a **busybody** in other people's matters"* (1 Pet. 4:15) (emphasis added). The idea of a "busybody" is also found in 1 Tim. 5:13: *"And besides they learn to be idle, wandering about from house to house, and not only idle but also gossips and **busybodies**, saying things which they ought not"* (emphasis added). The Greek word for *busybodies* is *periergos* (Strong's #4021) and can be interpreted as "curious arts." In the neuter plural form of this word, the definition is *magic*. It is as if a person can weave a spell over another person by being a busybody (curious arts, magic). While we often think of a female as being busybody, the Bible does not differentiate by gender. A male, as well as a female, can fall into this trap and become a tool of the devil (see also 2 Thess. 3:11).

3. The Complainer—*One who finds fault, a faultfinder.*

This type of person often uses a personal situation as a platform for their complaint. "I was treated unfairly." "Do you know what this person did?" or, "You think that's bad, let me tell you what happened to me." The problem with the complainer is they share from a personal perspective which creates an atmosphere of emotions and sympathy for their cause. Our willingness to listen leads to a greater opportunity to be defiled and contaminated by this person. We must separate our emotional connections to the complainer and recognize the violation of our spirits by the complaining individual. "*Now when the people* complained, *it displeased the Lord; for the Lord heard it, and His anger was aroused...*" (Num. 11:1) (emphasis added). God will not condone nor bless the complaining spirit. The complainer's motivation is to gain an advantage, be it spiritual, emotional or mental. Be aware of their subtle (and not so subtle) ways of drawing you into their way of thinking (see also Jude 16).

4. The Murmurer—*One who grumbles, a grumbler.*

We find that this person is usually complaining, but only loudly enough for those in *close* proximity to hear. In fact, it may be so soft that a nearby person inadvertently asks them to repeat the offensive comment. The murmuring person is seldom happy or pleased with the outcome of situations. They, like the complainer, look for faults and then justify a bad attitude with their comments. Consistent with His focus, God speaks clearly to this type of behavior, *"Do all things without **murmurings** and disputings"* (Phil. 2:14, KJV) (emphasis added). One of the clearest examples in scripture of complaining and murmuring is found in the 16th chapter of Numbers. This is the story of Korah and his rebellion against Moses. How did Korah get so many people to agree with him? The Bible tells us that these were not just people of the congregation, but they were "leaders, men of renown"(16:2). Can't you see it happening? Perhaps Korah was jealous of Moses and Aaron. Maybe Korah wanted more authority, recognition or power. Regardless of his motives, his methods are easily discerned. "Moses never treats us fairly." A person walking by might say, "What was that Korah?" Once we identify these people, their methods, their intent, their ways become clear to us. Korah simply went about poisoning the people and contaminating as many leaders *as would listen to him*. The end result was death to all those who opposed Moses and therefore they opposed God. How grateful and relieved must have been the people who said, "Korah, you are murmuring and I will not be a party to that type of conversation." especially after Korah and his group were swallowed by the earth. They were as relieved as you will be after your next encounter with a murmurer and complainer (see also Jude 16).

5. **The Slanderer**—*An individual who tries to injure someone's reputation or character by sharing damaging situations or stories.*

*"And the men, which Moses sent to search the land, who returned, and made all the congregation to murmur against him, by bringing up a **slander** upon the land"* (Num. 14:36, KJV) (emphasis added). The word used in this scripture for *slander* is the Hebrew word *dibbah*, which specifically means "evil report." Jeremiah speaks of those who slander in referring to the neighboring lands *"They are all stubborn rebels, walking as **slanderers**"* (Jer. 6:28) (emphasis added). This particular word means "scandal monger." An individual who slanders people is scandalous in God's eyes. This type of person may want to destroy or defame a reputation in order to be elevated in business, recognition or honor. The slanderer cannot be trusted to give accurate information as their sole purpose appears to be a self-serving message. Again, they defile and contaminate those who listen to their speech. It is for this reason that Paul includes the admonition about slanderers when speaking of the qualifications of a deacon. *"Likewise, their wives must be reverent, not **slanderers**, temperate, faithful in all things"* (1 Tim. 3:11) (emphasis added). Solomon, the wisest man in the land, wrote about the slanderer in Proverbs 10:18. He did not mince words, but stated very clearly, *"Whoever hides hatred has lying lips, and whoever spreads **slander** is a fool"* (emphasis added) (see also Psa. 101:5; Jer. 9:4).

6. **The Talebearer (or gossip)**—*A person who elaborates and exaggerates so as to make a story more dramatic (or juicy).*

   *"A **talebearer** revealeth secrets; but he that is of a faithful spirit concealeth the matter"* (Prov. 11:13, KJV) (emphasis added). God speaks seriously about the consequences and repercussions for those involved in an

evil report. Likewise, He gives us specific, clear guidelines to follow in our lives so as to avoid the pitfalls of the above habit patterns. Leviticus 19:16, in speaking about the covenantal laws of morality, states *"You shall not go about as a **talebearer** among your people; nor shall you take a stand against the life of your neighbor: I am the Lord"* (emphasis added). Romans 1:28-30 describes the situation where people refused to acknowledge the authority of God in their lives. Their refusal to honor, to worship and give thanks to the Lord, led God to turn them over to their own sinful natures:

Since these people refused even to think about God, He let their useless minds rule over them. That's why they do all sorts of indecent things. They are evil, wicked, and greedy, as well as mean in every possible way. They want what others have, and they murder, argue, cheat, and are hard to get along with. They gossip, say cruel things to others, and hate God (CEV).

If we associate with gossips and talebearers, we begin to become "loose" with our own tongue. The willingness to gossip and "discuss" other people becomes more a matter of habit than of a conscious choice. The more we are exposed to this area, the more contaminated we become in our spirits. The Hebrew word for *gossip* and *talebearer* is closely associated with the word used for a *whisperer* (see # 7 in this list). (See also Prov. 18:8, 20:19, 26:20, 26:22, 1 Tim. 5:13.)

7. **The Whisperer**—*An individual who privately, secretly and covertly talks about other people.*

Most of us have experienced the pain of the whisperer. This person uses the soft, hushed voice to secretly plot a demise of another's character or reputation.

Proverbs 16:28 states, *"A perverse man sows strife, and a **whisperer** separates the best of friends."* A whisper seems so innocent, so casual, even innocuous, yet it can destroy a person as it spreads like a wildfire. One way the word, *whisperer,* is used can be found in Psalm 41:7 when David writes, *"All who hate me **whisper** together against me; Against me they devise (plot) my hurt"* (emphasis added). The Hebrew word *lachash* is used in this context for *whisperer.* It means to "mumble a spell (as a magician)—a charmer" (Strong's # 3907). When I read this, it was a wake up call. I realized that there may be people who are cursing* me and casting a spell over me via their whispers. I am now able to engage in a spiritual warfare against such words.

I recently had dinner at a Chinese restaurant. At the end of the meal, I opened my fortune cookie and it read, "Speak only well of people and you need never whisper." While I don't put any merit in the *fortune* part of the cookie, I do think the person who wrote this particular statement was very wise.

Notice how many of the words, from the above seven examples, were linked together by their Greek or Hebrew roots. Take note of the words which were connected to spells or magic. This is witchcraft, plain and simple. We must begin to see evil reports for what they are —manipulation, curses, spells, accusations, magic...again, WITCHCRAFT! We must avoid, pray against and educate those around us as to the pitfalls the enemy has placed

---

* The area of blessing and cursing is spoken of throughout the Bible (Ps. 10:7, Ps. 59:12, Rom. 3:14). It is important to guard our lips against speaking negative or evil of another (cursing). There is power in our words. *"Out of the same mouth proceed blessing and cursing. My brethren, these things ought not to be so"* (Jam. 3:10).

before us. These pitfalls may not be adultery, gambling, alcohol, drugs, pornography or divorce—they are simply the words spoken by those around us—however, they are every bit as dangerous and deadly as any other pitfall that Satan may place in our path.

It is imperative for us to remember that *we are not always* the innocent little lambs who are being attacked by the big, bad evil reporter wolf. I remember a few years back when the one who was doing the defiling was me. It was a time when I was involved in coaching at the junior high school level. One of the teacher/coaches I worked with lacked in some areas of responsibility, which made working with him rather tiresome. It was well known among the staff (and even the district) that Jim (fictitious name) had an anger problem and was not the most responsible or organized individual. During the course of one week as I was talking with a supervisor about my coaching experience, we began to talk about Jim, and in a joking manner, went through a few of his escapades in past months and years. As we continued, I began to recount some of my most recent frustrations with Jim and the supervisor, likewise, shared his frustrations.

Later that evening, as I mulled over my part of the conversation, I realized that I had polluted the supervisor due to my speaking negatively about Jim. Please understand, everything I said was true. He was late to practice; he wasn't organized; he did leave early; and he did lack certain people skills. However, it was not my place, nor my responsibility to systematically address each of his shortcomings, with the clear intent to "injure his reputation." Fortunately, my discussion did not cause further damage to his reputation, but I am called to be a light, to speak with a spirit of truth and humility. Yet, as I examined my motivation and my heart, I realized that there was some malice and frustration in my conversation. I had defiled the supervisor and defrauded Jim. I was a whisperer, a complainer and a slanderer. Worse, I had failed to be a witness of Christianity in the midst of a secular system.

The next day I contacted the supervisor. I asked for his forgiveness for saying negative things about Jim. His response was one of shock and confusion. You see, in his eyes, we did nothing wrong. The people around us were used to cutting one another down and picking each other apart like vultures. When I apologized, he told me there was no need to say I was sorry. However, I knew better, so I repeated myself and explained that my speaking was not Christ-like and did not create a positive environment nor did it help Jim. After further discussion and testimony, the supervisor thanked me for my willingness to "take a stand." His appreciation for my honesty and intentions to create a godly atmosphere in the workplace were well received. I also developed a new prayer burden for Jim.

This incident took place many years ago, yet I will never forget it. I saw myself in a way that embarrassed me and which, I know, must have grieved the Holy Spirit. Sadly, this was not the last time I caught myself in this type of scenario, but the times of my defiling others is diminishing. I am still quick to repent and ask for forgiveness, and fortunately, I am then cleansed and freed from the condemnation of the enemy. I recently saw Jim and the above incident was brought back to my memory. Gratefully, I am increasing in my self-control and not allowing the devil to use me as a tool of his torture.

We must properly prepare our spirits and minds to protect ourselves from these traps. In the same way that

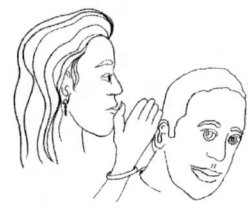 touching something diseased will defile one's hand, listening to an evil report will defile one's mind. The seriousness of and the guidelines and consequences for an evil (false) report are consistent throughout the scriptures.

*You shall not circulate a **false report**. Do not put your hand with the wicked to be an unrighteous witness.*

Exod. 23:1 (emphasis added)

*And the men, which Moses sent to search the land, who returned, and made all the congregation to **murmur** against him, by bringing up a **slander** upon the land, Even those men that did bring up the **evil report** upon the land, died by the plague before the Lord.*

Num. 14:37, KJV (emphasis added)

Obviously, this last scripture uses several of the key words and examples which we have previously discussed. Even the people who did not bring the evil report, but merely listened and did not come against it were killed. It is only by God's grace that I haven't been destroyed for my defilement of others as well as my unwillingness to take a stand against words of slander and gossip.

The third stairstep occurs when we are exposed to the negative aspects and attitudes of others, become confused and contaminated in our spirit, and enter into *foolish practices and responses*. The Bible reveals this pattern over and over again in the lives of spiritual people. This is an important point. We are not talking about an individual who does not have faith or knowledge of God, who is void of spiritual ethics and morality. No, we are referring to people who are believers in God and who have a history of drawing strength from Him. It is the people who have walked with God and have experienced His power and blessings who succumb to the subtle, devious distractions of Satan.

The Foolishness of Aaron

The subtle seduction of a spiritual person is indeed a sad arena to encounter, but unless we prepare ourselves for the vile ways of the enemy, this pattern will continue among the people of God. In the Book of Exodus, we can read about Aaron and his tendency to become "confused," "contaminated," and move into areas of "foolishness." Aaron saw, first-hand, the faithfulness and power of God. He was able to be a part of God's miracles and a testimony to the certainty of the Word of God. Despite the constant haranguing of Pharaoh, Aaron was able to be steadfast and support Moses in the deliverance of the Hebrew people.

Unfortunately, once the people were out of Egypt, the spirit of doubt began to creep into their spirits.

> *And when Pharaoh drew near, the children of Israel lifted their eyes, and behold, the Egyptians marched after them. So they were very afraid, and the children of Israel cried out to the Lord. Then they said to Moses, "Because there were no graves in Egypt, have you taken us away to die in the wilderness? Why have you so dealt with us, to bring us up out of Egypt? Is this not the word that we told you in Egypt, saying, let us alone that we may serve the Egyptians? For it would have been better for us to*

> *serve the Egyptians than that we should die in the wilderness."*
>
> Exod. 15:10-12

Aaron heard the complaints of the people. Was he also fearful? Did he become confused? The Bible doesn't tell us how Aaron reacted, but it does tell us that Moses responded with courage and boldness. Aaron witnessed the marvelous parting of the Red Sea and the miraculous salvation of the Israelites. But, I believe, something lingered in Aaron, beginning a seed of confusion which would come to fruition in subsequent situations.

In Exodus 16:2, 3, the children of Israel again begin to murmur:

> *Then the whole congregation of the children of Israel complained against Moses and Aaron in the wilderness. And the children of Israel said to them, "Oh, that we had died by the hand of the Lord in the land of Egypt, when we sat by the pots of meat and when we ate bread to the full! For you have brought us out into this wilderness to kill this whole assembly with hunger."*

Could this murmuring and whining affect Aaron? Certainly he loved God and was strengthened by the miracles constantly unfolded in front of him. When the manna continued to bless the people for many years, would this not have been enough to quiet the complaints of the people and show Aaron that these types of negative reports and comments carried no validity in the sight of God? Somewhere along the line, these words of doubt, complaining and murmuring impacted Aaron. He became confused, contaminated, and eventually, allowed the pressures from the people to move him into the level of foolishness. When did this happen, you might be thinking? Two words will remind you, golden calf!

The situation with the golden calf shows us the susceptible spirit which Aaron had when he relented to the pressure from people. Remember what took place? Moses was on Mt. Sinai receiving the Ten Commandments. While Moses was in the midst of the Glory of God, the people became impatient. An interesting note, when people become impatient, confusion often enters into the thinking process. They feel that they must solve the problem, avoiding God's timing and the direction of the Holy Spirit. Moses delayed in coming down. The people became nervous and wanted an idol built so they could worship God. Aaron relented and gathered up all the gold, and they made the idol of the calf. The gold they had was all from Egypt. They were slaves and had no possessions. Before leaving Egypt, they had received silver, gold and clothing from the Egyptians. The people of Israel were using the treasures of Egypt to erect an idol like the ones which had been worshipped in Egypt.

Moses came down from Mt. Sinai and saw the people dancing and praying to the calf.

> *And Moses said to Aaron, "What did this people do to you that you have brought so great a sin upon them?" So Aaron said, "Do not let the anger of my lord become hot. You know the people, that they are set on evil." For they said to me, "Make us gods that shall go before us; as for this Moses, the man who brought us out of the land of Egypt, we do not know*

what has become of him."

Exod. 32:21-23

Notice that Moses asked, *"What did the people do to you?"* He recognized that Aaron had been defiled by the interactions with the people and, with the usual defensiveness of a guilty person, Aaron responds by blaming the people and their evil nature. The first words out of Aaron's mouth should have been, "God, will you forgive me? And Moses, will you forgive me?" Aaron had become contaminated by the previous interactions and when confronted, in Moses's absence by the negative reports, he was unable to endure their caustic nature.

This is how the level of foolishness occurs. We allow previous experiences to influence us. "Sandy has been having a rough time and last week she was mad at me. So this time, I won't confront her and I'll go along with her. What she said wasn't very nice, but it doesn't happen too often. I'll just love her." If you love her, you will **not** go along with her. If an incident occurs once, it will likely be repeated unless there is an intervention of prevention.

It would be nice if Aaron could be a testimony and an example of one who learned his lesson. Wouldn't it be wonderful to say that Aaron never was confused or contaminated again—that in the future, the stage of "foolishness" was not attained and that Aaron made wise decisions? Unfortunately, as it so often occurs in our lives, it takes multiple encounters with pain and sin to truly get us to know, "When you play with fire, it is easy to get burned."

Let's examine a little more of Aaron's life.

There were many times when the people complained to Moses (and Aaron). In Numbers 11, we find a time when

God was so displeased with the complaining that He created fire to burn part of the camp. Once again, this murmuring and complaining created a questionable spirit within Aaron. We find this impacting him in the next chapter of Numbers.

> *Then Miriam and Aaron spoke against Moses because of the Ethiopian woman whom he had married; for he had married an Ethiopian woman. So they said, "Has the Lord indeed spoken only through Moses? Has He not spoken through us also?" And the Lord heard it. Now the man Moses was very humble, more than all men who were on the face of the earth.*
>
> Num. 12:1-3

In verse one, the word, *spoke*, means "to subdue or to destroy." Aaron was making an evil report against Moses. Aaron, having been affected by the congregation of Israel, now takes up his own offense and defiles others. This is the pattern of evil reports—cyclical. I share something of an evil nature, you become contaminated. In your foolishness, you share a negative report and someone else gets contaminated. This repeats itself until the enemy has sufficiently divided a place of business, a family, friends and the Body of Christ.

The classic example of the cyclical pattern of a false or negative report is found in Numbers 13. The story of the spies who went into Canaan only serves to illustrate the danger of allowing the repetitive nature of evil reports. Even though God told Moses, and the people, that the land of Canaan was being given to them, many of the people had already been contaminated and defiled. They were confused and uncertain as to the truth of the promises laid before them. The story is tragic and has been told countless times. Of the twelve spies who saw the land, only two came back with an accurate report. Both Caleb and Joshua saw the land through spiritual eyes, while the others saw the land through defiled and deceived eyes. *"And they brought up an evil report of the land which they had searched unto the children of Israel..."* (Num. 13:32, KJV). Due to the constant murmuring and negative comments which had infiltrated the Israelite's lives, many of the people were not thinking clearly and were operating out of fear. (I will discuss this further in a later chapter.) When we are saturated by negative and false reports, our defense mechanism begins to become weary. We begin to see situations through clouded eyes and it is easy to misinterpret the intentions of people, to misread the actions of a situation, or to become overwhelmed emotionally.

We find another example of murmuring and defilement in Numbers 16 as we examine the story of Korah.

> *Now Korah the son of Izhar, the son of Kohath, the son of Levi, with Dathan and Abiram the sons of Eliab, and On the son of Peleth, sons of Reuben, took men; and they rose up before Moses with some of the children of Israel, two hundred and fifty leaders of the congregation, representatives of the congregation, men of renown. They gathered together against Moses and Aaron, and said to them, "You take too much upon yourselves, for all the congregation is holy, every one of them, and the Lord is among them. Why then do you exalt yourselves above the assembly of the Lord?" So when Moses heard it, he fell on his face...*
>
> Num. 16:1-4

Again, we find that Korah and the others had been exposed to the murmuring and gossiping of the people of

Israel. This constant negative input created a distortion in their spirit which led to eventually coming against Moses and Aaron. It should be very clear that simply standing by and listening, but not participating in the evil report, does not protect one's mind or spirit from being infected.

Korah and his colleagues wanted recognition for themselves. Their cry, "Recognize me!" was heard throughout the congregation. This type of self-serving and selfish focus is a constant stumbling block to fellowship with God. We find this egocentric, self-focused attitude infiltrating the minds and hearts of many believers. This has been a battle throughout history as we look at Cain, Jacob, King Saul, Absalom, Samson, Martha and Judas. Of course, the names could be more contemporary and the list could be Mike, Tom, Sarah, Mary, Jim, Carol, Sandy, or Brian. Our attempts to elevate self only lead to the building of idols in our lives. This is foolishness and prevents us from growing in our relationship with Christ.

People who are involved in defiling other people, often seek to glorify self and flesh. It is essential that we are wise in the strategies of this type of person so we don't become part of the ungodly memorial in their life. Will your life be memorialized by "you"—by a monument you build by hands—or by the godly character and actions of your life, prayer, servanthood, grace, mercy, compassion, godly standards and uncompromising integrity? Take a moment and ask God if you have any self-made monuments which need to be destroyed. Our repentance and willingness to submit to Christ will bring about purification in our lives.

QUESTIONS—Examining the Heart

1. What legacy or memorial are you leaving behind? Make a list of those qualities of God you wish to have displayed in your life.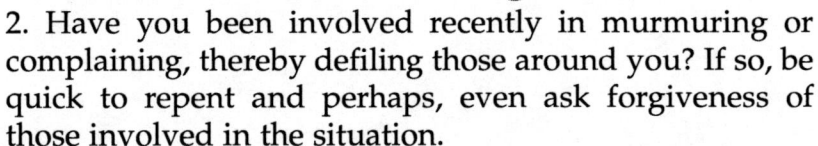

2. Have you been involved recently in murmuring or complaining, thereby defiling those around you? If so, be quick to repent and perhaps, even ask forgiveness of those involved in the situation.

3. Are there people around you who have created a subtle influence on you? Like Aaron, have you found yourself doing or saying "foolish" things which lead to areas of destruction?

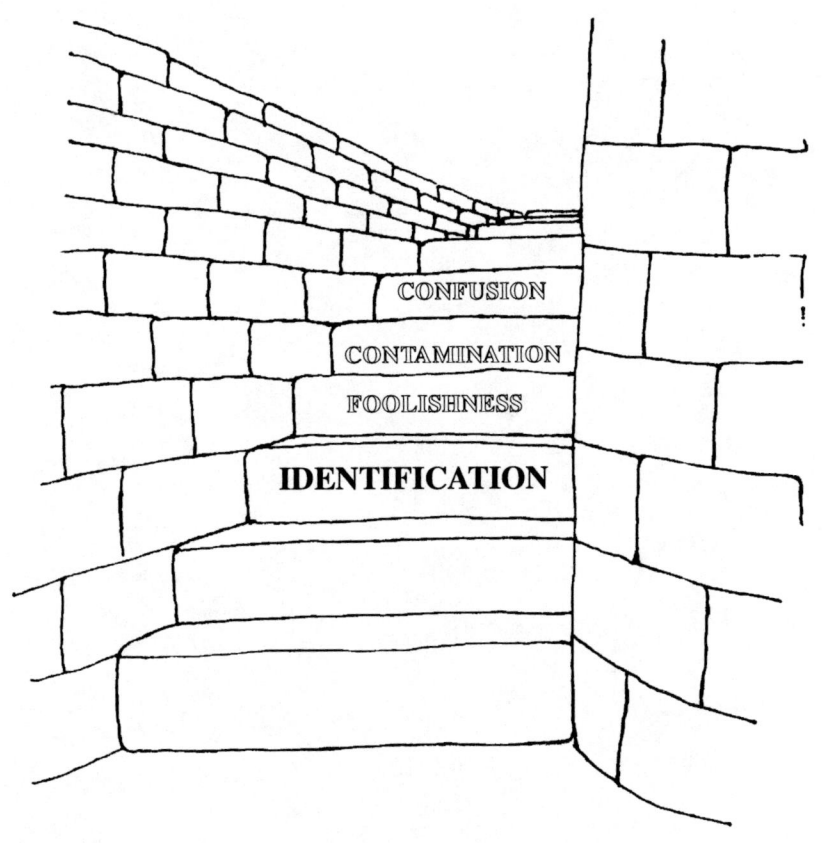

CHAPTER 7

IDENTIFICATION

Have you ever had a conversation with someone and as the conversation progressed, one of you commented, "We really have a lot in common"? The conversation may have been focused on jobs, interests, family, personal likes or dislikes. Regardless, something struck a cord of agreement between the two of you. This type of occurrence may be the beginning of a new friendship or relationship. There seems to be something within most of us that is looking for someone to agree with us. It may be due to our own insecurity, our need for affirmation, a need for encouragement or even a vote of confidence.

The next time you are in a meeting or among a group of people, take note of the nonverbal approach of the speaker. His or her tendency will be to scan the audience for a listening ear. Once this has been established, the speaker will often times "lock in" on that person, as if they are the only one in the room. Try this yourself when someone is sharing. Maintain strong eye contact with the speaker. (No, don't stare at them with laser eyes.) Nod your head in support and agreement, even smile when appropriate. You will find the speaker zeroing in on you more often. They have found an ally, someone to affirm them during their time of sharing. This type of connection is used as a tool by those who give evil reports.

I am not sharing this with you so we can do experiments on people in group settings, as if they were laboratory rats. I can just hear it, "Hey, tomorrow in church, let's stare at Pastor Thomas and see if he will stare back at us."

The poor minister will feel like he entered the Twilight Zone. "Hey Martha," he might say to his wife, "could you believe all those eyes bugging out. My sermon must have really been a winner." So let me be clear, my previous discussion regarding group dynamics was only an illustration (Hey! Quit staring at me).

Seriously, people relate to those who affirm them. I am attempting to help each reader realize the power of agreement and the need within us for identification. We draw strength from one another and utilize the agreement among us as a way to affirm our positions, attitudes and conversations. It is not uncommon to gravitate toward people who agree with us and even advocate our position and beliefs. There are certain ones who like to connect with people of a contrary position. (Don't you just love a good argument, *especially* when you're right?) Fortunately, this is usually dependent upon the situation and not a common tendency in most people.

Some years ago, I was speaking to a group of professional people on the subject of "teenagers." This was a secular setting so the ideas and opinions were very diversified, but definitely leaning toward a more liberal viewpoint regarding acceptable behavior. The subject of sexual behavior and promiscuity was brought forth from the audience. Several comments were made regarding health clinics in schools and the availability of birth control within the public school setting. After several minutes of general discussion, one of the participants asked for my opinion. Being the shy, demure person that I am (wink, wink) I hesitated for a moment as I surveyed the crowd. It was apparent this subject was one with a strong emotional base. After a moment or two, I ventured forth with my answer. "I find it rather curious and even disconcerting," I said, "that we, as a society, hand out condoms, birth control pills and needles to people and tell them to act responsibly when we have never taken the time to teach these same people how to be responsible." The array of facial expressions included glares, stares, smiles, head shaking and grimaces, among many others. I continued, "We allow abortions without parental approval yet do little to facilitate parent-child communication. Children are told to be involved in 'safe sex' and 'drive responsibly—if you drink, don't drive,' but our societal framework teaches promiscuity, 'if it feels good—do it, you are only accountable to yourself.'" Needless to say, as I talked, the majority of the people were, shall we say, not in agreement with me. I continued to share my heart and began searching the crowd for a friendly face, a nod of support or eye contact without the dagger stare. I must have looked like a scared deer caught in the headlights. All I wanted was a reassuring look or smile of affirmation. When the day was over, while I had one or two people make negative comments, I received many written and verbal messages indicating appreciation for my comments. While no one in the audience vocalized identification with my comments during the workshop, there were many that inwardly agreed with me. Honestly, I sure could have used a few brave souls who would have vocally supported me.

This type of connection has tremendous ramifications when relating it to "evil reports." When we place ourselves in the position of hearing a negative conversation regarding someone, our flesh seeks for identification. While I may not consciously want to agree, my soul hangs on every word, searching the memory banks of my mind and emotions for similar experiences and feelings. "Yes, I know that type of hurt." I find myself thinking and, perhaps, my lips vocalizing these words. This fourth stairstep of defilement, **identification**, is a powerful bond between people. Rather, I should say, a powerful *bondage* when used to unite people surrounding an evil report.

IDENTIFICATION: Emotionally, intellectually or spiritually connecting with another individual.

Does this really happen that often? Are we really "pulled into" discussions by our commonalities? Without hesitation, the answer to these questions is unequivocally—YES!! Identification may be a positive area when we draw godly strength and guidance from another individual. Our desire may be to empathize with people, but, if we are not careful, we may end up being tantalized, spiritually pulverized and eventually demoralized by this seductive process. True, effective empathy has the ability to examine a situation from another's perspective without becoming emotionally, mentally or spiritually distorted in the viewpoint. But, so often, what begins as an attempt at empathy quickly becomes sympathy and feeling sorry for an individual. We try to make people feel better by sharing our own stories and areas of identification. Soon, we are trapped in a web of confusion, which leads to deceit and deception. This is the subtlety of **identification**.

I grew up in Phoenix, Arizona, during the times of the turbulent 1960s. Throughout the country, there were marches for freedom, protests, race riots and polarization due to the Vietnam War. It was a time that began to tear at the very core of our nation. No longer were the police, armed services or military people and government officials seen as people above reproach. Questions abounded amongst the people. Parents and children were separated by ideology and a great chasm existed between generations. Still, in the midst of all this turmoil, people had a need for "identification." Two factions began to emerge in relations to political beliefs regarding Vietnam—The Hawks and The Doves. The Hawks were ones who were more aggressive, more interested in *winning* the war, even at an extreme cost. The bombing of Vietnam and increasing military numbers and action in the country were among several supported ideas from the midst of this group. On the other side, the Doves were passive, believing we should never have entered Vietnam. The doves believed war was wrong. We were not to be in another country, having Americans killed. This was different from World War II during which Pearl Harbor was attacked. This was a tiny country, not even associated with us.*

---

* The author recognizes that these explanations are incomplete and limited. However, the intent is to use an illustration, not develop a political science framework. Apologies for the finite explanation.

For over ten years, the debate raged. People were torn in their allegiances. In my own home, I had a brother fighting in Vietnam as part of the Marine Corps. Yet another brother was wearing black armbands and protesting the war. As you can imagine, family gatherings were very, very interesting. Accusations, criticism and attacks were rampant throughout homes, neighborhoods, cities and the nation. And, here was I, a young teenager, who did not have a political bone in my body. Well, that is not exactly true, as I was junior class vice-president and senior class president. Rumor had it that my main motivation for running for political office was to get out of class and get special privileges. I emphatically deny that charge...it wasn't my *main* motivation, but it did weigh heavily on my decisions.

The teenage years were challenging enough without the emotional fear and psychological factor of potentially being drafted into the service, spending your birthdays and holidays in a fox hole, far away from home. The pressure (and need) to identify with one of the groups, Hawks or Doves, was great. The newspaper, radio and television were all full of political innuendoes, slanted reporting and bandwagon approaches. Which group would a person join? The impact and ramifications would carry into the school and community. It was a discussion which came up weekly, if not daily. It dominated the classroom discussions in history, english and even math, depending on the day's occurrence in Vietnam. Graphic pictures and stories of the war bombarded the airwaves. This was the first military encounter that was exposed on the airwaves. It was as if you were there when each bomb exploded, each person was shot, and another father was taken away from a son and daughter or a son/daughter stolen from a parent.

As I look back on those days, I realize the number of false reports which were given. People, in an attempt to color my views, would lie, change the facts and deceive in an effort to garner support. One teacher, who felt we should not be in Vietnam, would share gory and painful stories about the suffering of the Vietnamese children and non-military people. Another educator would share how the servicemen and women were being tortured and injured by "innocent civilians" who were only a front for the military regime.

Evil and distorted reports were a constant part of the battle of words taking place during the Vietnam era. Today, I am a little unclear as to what I would do differently in some areas. One thing though, which is very clear, is that I would not rely on the reports of others to gain my identification. I would do more research, find out the truth for myself. It was too easy to rely on the information of so-called experts. Avoid the trap of falling into emotional identification by getting information for yourself. Compare your feelings and thoughts with the Bible. Look for corroboration or contradictions in your assessment of the situation. And finally, for those in your life who have been faithful, trustworthy and proven themselves as people of integrity, weigh their perspective a little heavier than a stranger or apparent "expert" without a track record of honesty.

I know I am not alone in my tendency to want to listen to the advice of others. There are many times when my confidence is shaken and I look for guidance from others. Unfortunately, I do not always pray and ask the Father's guidance nor do I always seek out godly counsel. Again, obtaining counsel is good, but whom do you seek it from in life. Once you become aware of the pitfalls of false reports, it is easier to discern when one is attempting to manipulate and control your thinking. An evil report has a strong aroma, one that is overpowering when stated with a passion. The "sherman tank" approach (I will run over you with my words) is common among people and is found throughout the Bible. But, some people use a more subtle, seductive approach. Like a sniper, they come out of nowhere, cause injury, and retreat before being recognized. A classic example of this is found in 2 Samuel 15:1-6:

> *After this it happened that Absalom provided himself with chariots and horses, and fifty men to run before him. Now Absalom would rise early and stand beside the way to the gate. So it was, whenever anyone who had a controversy came to the king for a decision, that Absalom would call to him and say, "What city are you from?" And he would say, "Your servant is from such and such a tribe of Israel." Then Absalom would say to him, "Look, your case is good and right; but there is no listener of the king to hear you." Moreover Absalom would say, "Oh, that I were made judge in the land, and everyone who has any suit or cause would come to me; then I would give him justice." And so it was, whenever anyone came near to bow down to him, that he would put out his hand and take him and kiss him. In this manner Absalom acted toward all Israel who came to the king for judgment. So Absalom stole the hearts of the men of Israel.*

Absalom used an innocent-sounding evil report (now there is an oxymoron for you **"an innocent evil report"**) to turn the hearts and affections of almost an entire nation and lead it in revolt against his own father, King David.

The "report" emphasized Absalom's "care and concern" for the hurting people, his "righteous desire" that justice be done and his "ability" to be a better administrator than his father. While it may appear that Absalom was a power monger, desiring to usurp his father's authority for the sake of his own ego, the truth lies in the fact that David was not a loving father to Absalom. David was guilty of poor parenting decisions which affected his son. It caused bitterness and rejection in Absalom that eventually surfaced as anger and rebellion.

The heart-wrenching breach between David and his son is found in 2 Samuel, chapters 13 and 14. Absalom had a sister named Tamar. Tamar was raped by her half-brother Amnon. David was angry, yet took no action against the violation of Tamar by Amnon. The years passed and Absalom exacted revenge for his sister by having Amnon murdered. Out of fear of reprisal by his father David, Absalom fled the area for several years. Even though Absalom returned to Jerusalem (2 Sam. 14), David did not embrace his son, nor show love and affection to him. David did not reach out to him for two years. It was not until Joab went to King David, on behalf of Absalom, that David met with his son. Even then, it was hardly a meeting of reconciliation. David did not extend forgiveness—the forgiveness that would have healed a scared, broken young man. This created a wound in Absalom and he wanted to seek revenge against his father for the hurt.

The events surrounding Absalom and David may seem extreme, but the results are very typical when people are wounded in life. One becomes hurt by another. There is no clear reconciliation, and bitterness begins to creep into a life. Oh yes, the injured person says they are okay, but the seed of rejection and hurt begins to grow. It soon monopolizes their outlook on life, the way they relate to family, friends and situations. The emotionally injured person seeks out others to align (or identify) with them and as a result, each person they speak to may become poisoned and pick up an offense. Absalom was very effective at "sharing the wealth" of his bitterness with others. We can learn how to avoid this type of person by further examining his approach.

Stealing the Hearts of the People

- 2 Samuel 15:1 *"After this it happened that Absalom provided himself with chariots and horses, and fifty men to run before him."* Quickly, Absalom found fifty others to identify with his plight. Individuals who use evil reports to discredit others will try to find people to agree with them. By surrounding himself with other people, Absalom felt justified and empowered to come against the king. It is important to be wary of people who obtain others to validate their displeasure with a situation as they will often step back and allow the "followers" to become the scapegoats, if problems arise. And as often happens, Absalom placed those people as a safeguard between the King and himself. (They ran before him.) King Saul is an example of one who used scapegoating (using people to protect his own sinful nature.) This is found in 1 Sam. 15, when he chose not to kill King Agag and the Amalekites. There were clear instructions to Saul regarding his attack on the Amalekites. However, he disobeyed the commands of God. When confronted by the prophet Samuel regarding the animals, jewelry and possessions, King Saul responded by blaming the people.

> *They have brought them from the Amalekites; for the people spared the best of the sheep and the oxen, to sacrifice to the Lord your God; and the rest we have utterly destroyed.*
>
> 1 Sam. 15:15

I find it interesting that the **king** is blaming the people for a decision made during the conquest of the Amalekites. Naturally, if there would have been praise and honor, the king would have directed that to the people, right? Hah! In actuality, the king would have patted himself on the back and taken the glory. If you are in any doubt as to whether this would have occurred, we find this type of account in 1 Samuel 15:13. Samuel, directed by God to confront King Saul, is met by an apparently joyful king. *"Then Samuel went to Saul, and Saul said to him, 'Blessed are you of the Lord! I have performed the commandment of the Lord.'"* Notice that Saul did not mention the people, but said "I have" not "we have." How quickly his story changed once it became evident that God was displeased with the situation. Evil reporters will protect themselves at the cost of another person's reputation, character or future.

- *Now Absalom would rise early and stand beside the way to the gate. So it was, whenever anyone who had a controversy came to the king for a decision, that Absalom would call to him and say, "What city are you from?" And he would say, "Your servant is from such and such a tribe of Israel."*

   2 Sam. 15:2

Absalom was smart; he chose people who had a grievance, people who already had a complaint. In chapter two of this book, I discussed how a carrier of an evil report will test your spirit for compatibility. We see that taking place in this passage. Absalom is attempting to connect with the people so he can then draw them alongside his own cause. His first attempts are to find some common ground of interest. This is usually how the stage of identification gains in power — through common hurts and frustrations. Absalom is appearing as a friendly neighbor asking personal questions, "small talk," to gain the confidence of the people.

- 2 Samuel 15:3 *"Then Absalom would say to him, 'Look, your case is good and right; but there is no listener of the king to hear you.'"* A carrier will do their best to sympathize with your situation, even to the point of supporting your grievance. They will pick up your offense and aid in substantiating your frustrations. Naturally, their hope is that you will identify and reciprocate by supporting their issues. This is clearly the case for Absalom as he wistfully comments about being king, in front of the people. He is attempting to engage with a sympathetic spirit. Please note, the people coming to the king were following the procedures of the land. If they had a grievance, they were to come to the king for a dispute resolution. However, each person coming to the king must have been upset, offended and feeling frustrated with their situation. Those of us who are prone to being offended are "ripe" for the enemy to come and pick us off.

- 2 Samuel 15:4 *"Moreover Absalom would say, 'Oh, that I were made judge in the land, and everyone who has any suit or cause would come to me; then I would give him justice.'"* This reminds me of the scene from the *Wizard of Oz* where the cowardly Lion is singing, "If I were the king of the forest..." Absalom offered to be the representative of the people, to make sure everything was being done fairly and correctly. Here the people began to be taken in by Absalom and his evil reports. These people had not even seen the King, but because of their propensity toward anger, Absalom was able to align their spirit with his spirit. Are we just looking for a sympathetic ear to agree with us or are we asking for people to speak the truth to us? I can remember many times being angry with someone because they spoke the truth to me. How about you? We respond in odd ways when the truth pierces the lie, when the light shatters the darkness. On each day that Absalom approached the bitter, frustrated people, they began to whisper, murmur and agree with the polluted, malcontent spirit from Absalom. Without even realizing what was happening, the people of the land became defiled. Absalom was encouraged by the results and continued to touch, contaminate and defile the people who came to see the king.

- 2 Samuel 15:5 *"And so it was, whenever anyone came near to bow down to him, that he would put out his hand and take him and kiss him."* Absalom was seeking acceptance and recognition. This continued each day, and Absalom grew in authority in the eyes of the people. The authority was illegal as it was usurped from the rightful leader. While David refused to take this authority from King Saul, David's own son was quick to receive this ungodly adoration. People who are involved with evil reports often have a skewed perspective in life and feel insecure. The antidote, in their mind and spirit, is carnal recognition. We call this pride and arrogance. Many years ago, in healing areas of my own life, God showed me that my pride and performance mentality was actually based on insecurity. Until I find my security in Christ, I will look for recognition from people, materialism, performance and other worldly ways. Of course, only repentance, deliverance and healing from God will truly cleanse our spirit.

- 2 Samuel 15:6 *"In this manner Absalom acted toward all Israel who came to the king for judgment. So Absalom stole the hearts of the men of Israel."* In the Contemporary English Version, we find it written as follows, *"That's how he treated everyone from Israel who brought a complaint to the king. Soon everyone in Israel liked Absalom better than they liked David."* Absalom carried out a tragic take-over of the nation with the help of those who were defiled and infected with an evil report. The foundation of Absalom's authority was based on deceit, mistrust, anger, bitterness and was spiritually illegal. Absalom was not given the authority by God; he latched onto the authority of men. 2 Samuel 18, tells us of the demise of Absalom and all he tried to hold onto in the natural. Absalom wanted to be recognized by men and attempted to steal the godly recognition given to David. In the end, the only way Absalom could be memorialized was by his own hand.

> *When Absalom was alive, he had set up a stone monument for himself in King's Valley. He explained, "I don't have any sons to keep my name alive." He called it Absalom's Monument, and that is the name it still has today.*
>
> 2 Sam. 18:18, CEV

It is fitting that Absalom's only testimony of his life was a monument he built to himself. In a later chapter, we will explore the accuracy of Absalom's statement regarding "having no sons." Absalom, like Korah, was looking for self-exaltation and approval from people. When we investigate our own motives in life, do we find areas of pride, selfishness and a need for recognition? Take a moment and ask God to expose those areas of your life which conflict with His servant desires for your life.

*"Dear Heavenly Father, please expose those areas of my life which are in contradiction to Your will for me. I release my own selfish desires for personal gain and recognition. It is You, and You alone, who can exalt us in pure ways. My ways are known to You, O Lord, and I ask for You to change **my** ways to **Your** ways. For Your ways are truly higher than my ways, just as Your thoughts are higher than my thoughts. Thank you for Your steadfast love and faithfulness. Amen."*

QUESTIONS—Examining the Heart

1. Are there people you usually talk to regarding certain situations because you will receive support and agreement from them?

2. Is there an Absalom in your life? Are there people, or a person, whom you have become sympathetic toward, and whom you are following toward destruction?

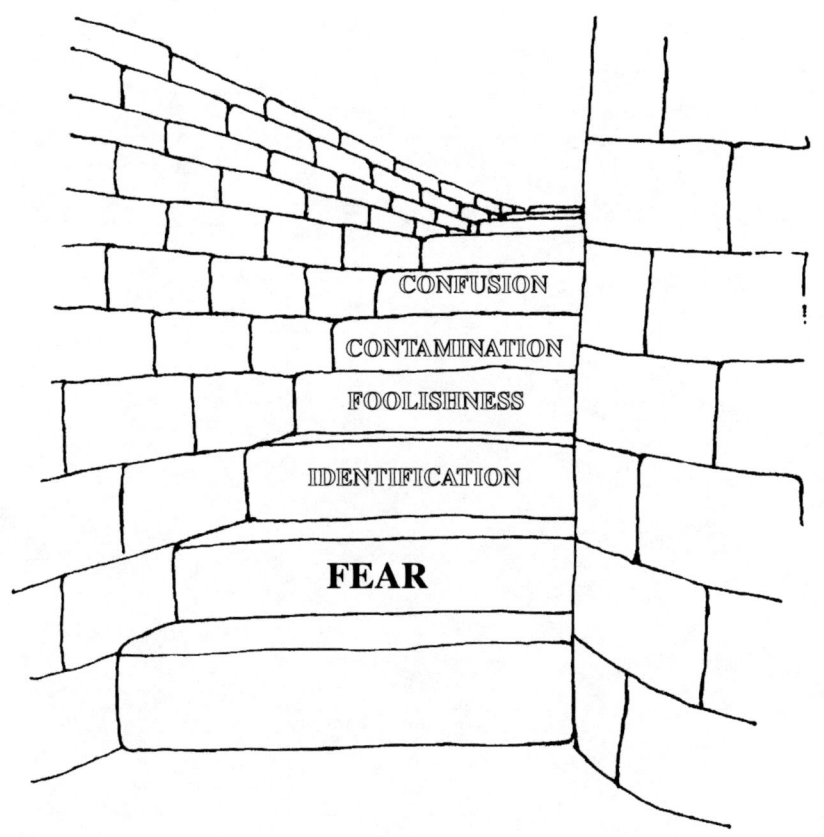

CHAPTER 8

FEAR

"In Germany, they came first for the Communists, and I didn't speak up because I wasn't a Communist. Then they came for the Jews, and I didn't speak up because I wasn't a Jew. Then they came for the trade unionists, and I didn't speak up because I wasn't a trade unionist. Then they came for the Catholics, and I didn't speak up because I was a Protestant. Then they came for me, and by that time, no one was left to speak."

Martin Niemoeller, 1892-1984

The Webster 1828 dictionary defines the word *fear* as a "painful emotion or passion excited by an expectation of evil. Fear is accompanied with a desire to avoid or ward off the expected evil. Fear is an uneasiness of mind, upon the thought of future evil likely to befall us." The idea of fear is one which grips us and causes us to respond with human thoughts, logic and emotions. It short circuits our spiritual discernment, mercy, compassion and love. This powerful emotion can create a panic or terror within us which is so great, we may respond to "normal" situations in outlandish ways, far beyond a reasonable response.

> **FEAR:** Anxiety-producing emotions that lead one to be concerned about losing control. This is often brought about by unexpected or poorly handled situations.

Fear is an emotion that can be equated to being teased— a little bit may feel okay, but the more it occurs, the more irritating it becomes and it eventually may move into the expression of anger. Remember as a child when a sibling or friend began tickling you? At first, you would laugh, but soon it became annoying, frustrating and you may have cried or started fighting. When we first feel the beginnings of fear, it may be stimulating, exciting. It may be somewhat like a roller coaster ride or a scary moment of a movie. But if fear persists in a life, it creates a tension so great that people say and do things they might not normally do. Fear is captivating and creates a cycle of confusion that may lead to a serious path of hurt, pain and destruction. **Fear** is our fifth stairstep or stage of defilement.

How can a false report about an individual create a fear response in us? What are the ways fear can grip us when we are a part of an evil report? Is it possible to break out of the fear cycle if we have been polluted by another person's conversation? The spiral of defilement is like a whirlpool of water. It is fascinating to look at and somewhat hypnotic, but if you get caught up in the current it is very difficult to get out. As we spin around and around in the whirlpool, all points of reference get blurred. The fear cycle is one which spins us around to such an extent that we cannot identify the beginning from the end. What was meant as an innocent comment is interpreted as a cutting remark. Simple conversations are distorted and convoluted in our mind. Paranoia creeps in and we begin to feel "everyone" is against us and is talking about us.

I remember swimming in the ocean during my college days. I loved the waves crashing against the shore, the taste of salt on my lips, the fresh smell of the sea. I spent many hours enjoying the sun, the surf and the sand. Naturally, this was *after* I had finished going to class, doing my homework and studying for every test I was going to take the next day. Well, maybe it was before, or instead of, I can't remember—it is such a (convenient) blur. Regardless of my personal study habits back then, this point is going to be poignant, so pay attention. At the beach, I specifically enjoyed "body surfing." I would swim out to where the waves began to grow, crest and then break (roll over themselves). As the waves began to grow, I swam toward the shore. The key was to swim at the exact time the wave crested. The momentum of the wave carried me toward the shore. When done properly, I could actually be in the midst of the wave, with my head out of the water, and enjoy a "free water ride."

Occasionally, the wave would suddenly break, roll over and crash down to the sand with me in the middle of the wave. My body would be thrust forcefully down to the sand. The turbulence of the water would spin me around, over and over again. When it happens, it becomes increasingly more difficult to tell which way is up and where the fresh air is going to be found. I remember the times when my lungs were ready to burst from need of  oxygen, yet my body was being tossed to and fro like a piece of seaweed. I frantically and desperately swam toward the surface only to realize I was swimming sideways or worse yet, toward the bottom. The feeling of panic and fear only magnified my confusion, my misdirection and my tendency to respond with fury. When I finally achieved the freedom from the watery prison, I took a few breaths then submitted myself to the torturous routine again, all for the purpose of "catching" the elusive big wave.

When we place ourselves in a position to converse with people regarding gossip and murmuring, the areas of confusion, contamination, foolishness and identification can all be a part of the defilement. However, it is the emotion of fear which opens up the door for the dangerous stairstep of impurity. (This stairstep will be discussed in the next chapter.) Fear creates a panic, a stress, which causes us to think that we must respond immediately with exceptional force and conviction. As in my ocean experiences, our perspective becomes distorted, we attempt to reach for "fresh air" only to realize we have gone in the wrong direction. This only reinforces the panicky emotions and elevates the desperate nature of our actions. If we continue to develop this pattern in our lives, each situation becomes more and more unclear as we react to people with confusion, judgment, criticism and condemnation.

I do recognize that there are times when fear is very good. Fear and anxiety may provide a caution or warning of imminent danger. It may make us more aware of our surroundings and a possible harmful atmosphere in life. A little child may be fearful to cross a busy street by herself. Another person may be fearful of walking alone in certain cities or areas. It is important to have an understanding of fear and the wisdom to know what to fear. We are instructed, by Scripture, to be fearful of God. That is, to honor, respect and be reverent of His power and authority. However, God never intended fear to be bondage in our life. It is intended to guide, keep us safe and under the protective covering of God.

To Fear or Not to Fear

- *"...when the Lord said to me, 'Gather the people to Me, and I will let them hear My words, that they may learn **to fear Me** all the days they live on the earth..."'* (Deut. 4:10) (emphasis added).

- *"The **fear of the Lord** is the beginning of knowledge, but fools despise wisdom and instruction"* (Prov. 1:7) (emphasis added).

- *"**Serve the Lord with fear**, And rejoice with trembling"* (Psa. 2:11) (emphasis added).

- *"The **fear of the Lord** is clean, enduring forever..."* (Psa. 19: 9a) (emphasis added).

- *"Honor all people. Love the brotherhood. **Fear God**. Honor the king"* (1 Peter 2:17) (emphasis added).

At the same time we are told to **have "fear" in God**; the Lord also commands us to **not have "fear" in man** or his evil ways.

- *"Yea, though I walk through the valley of the shadow of*

*death, I will **fear no evil**..."* (Psa. 23:4a) (emphasis added).

- *"**But do not fear**, O My servant Jacob...No one shall make him afraid"*(Jer. 46:27) (emphasis added).
- *"**Do not fear**, O Jacob My servant," says the Lord, "For I am with you"*(Jer. 46:28a) (emphasis added).

What is God saying in this apparent paradoxical approach? Are we to fear or not? How can we know when to fear? Is it okay to fear or not? I believe the key is found in the Scripture, *"In God (I will praise His word), in God I have put my trust; I will not fear. What can flesh do to me?"* (Psa. 56:4). The instructions and guidance given by God are very clear. Love God, hate evil. Trust in God, not in man. Fear the Lord; flee from evil. *"The fear of the Lord is to hate evil; Pride and arrogance and the evil way and the perverse mouth I hate"* (Prov. 8:13).

Unfortunately, in circumstances where false reports are being uttered, the "fear of the Lord" is usually missing. Our "trust" is then placed in the constant barrage of negative remarks, condescending glares and inaccurate information. This wears down our defenses and begins to take a terrible toll on us. As stated previously, our responses become atypical of us (as godly men or women), but typical of a defiled person. The tremendous danger of the "stairstep of fear" is its ability to have us reject the truth we know, the people we love and the destiny to which God has called us. We begin to anticipate negative outcomes. This can almost be a fixation. We anticipate accidents, broken relationships, injuries, rejection and hurt. Faith does not operate in the realm of fear. In fact, it could be said that fear is the opposite of faith. Remember the definition of fear shared earlier in this chapter. "...Fear is an uneasiness of mind, upon the thought of future evil likely to befall us." What are we dwelling on when we are in fear—God's goodness or gloom and doom?

It was during a recent time of ministry with a couple in our church that my wife, Joyce, and I saw the full effect of fear upon a marriage. The couple was struggling in their marriage and asked for counsel and prayer. Their problems were real and, in fact, very serious in nature. Even though the people shared in a way which gave little hope to their marriage, Joyce and I spoke faith and truth into their lives. We serve an awesome God whom we have seen take broken lives and marriages and restore them miraculously. At one point, Joyce pressed in a little deeper and asked for some clarification. "It seems you have made up your mind about your marriage," Joyce stated. "What kind of feedback have you had in regards to the future of your marriage?" This question was asking the couple to divulge the source(s) of input for their lives. Was it the Bible? Prayer? Godly counsel with friends, leadership, or ministry? Was it the next-door neighbor? A person at work? Another guy or gal going through (or having completed) similar trials?

The next few minutes were very telling in the lives of this couple. They both had listened to "friends" who had been divorced or were separated. That negative input had placed fear within the couple. They were confused and hurting. They both acknowledged the tendency to "identify" with the problems and negate the possibility of solutions. "My wife (or husband) does that too" was a common phrase.

May I tell you the phrase that tipped us off? We have heard it too many times, but whenever we hear it come from someone's mouth, we know they have been polluted by the world. This phrase tells us that God is not a part of their thinking and they have moved into a fear of the world, of life and of the future. The phrase is "I have given to others all my life and now I need to look out for myself." They are saying: "I no longer want to serve." "I am more important than anyone." "Meeting my partner's needs is not as important as meeting my own needs." Naturally, these thoughts are all biblical in their content and intent. Right? WRONG!! Negative! Do not pass Go! Do not collect 200 dollars! I will come back to this situation later in this chapter.

The Resurrection of Lazarus

Let us look at a biblical account involving Jesus and some very dear friends. Take note that constant negative and false reports greatly impacted the thinking of people in biblical times also. So much so, that they lost sight of who Jesus really is and of His authority. Mary and Martha were both dearly loved by Jesus. He had spent time at their house, both socializing and ministering. Mary had anointed the feet of Jesus with oil and wiped his feet with her hair. The Bible says, "Now Jesus loved Martha and her sister and Lazarus" (John 11:5). It is very evident that Mary, Martha and Lazarus had spent time with Jesus.

Through those times, they had "connected" and built relationships with one another. Of course, even in the midst of their time together, swirling around, in the air of conversation, were constant charges and allegations about Jesus. The city of Bethany, the home of Mary, Martha and Lazarus was an oppressed area. It was also known as "the house of misery" because of its reputation for welcoming many physically injured and emotionally hurting people. How many times were curses made toward Jesus regarding the assertion of His being "The Christ"? The Pharisees regularly challenged, belittled and besmirched the name of Jesus. Is it possible that after hearing these comments, even Mary, Martha and Lazarus got worn down? Could fear have been placed within them due to the persistent spirits of confusion and contamination which surrounded them daily?

In John, chapter 11, we read the account of Lazarus being ill, so the sisters sent a message to Jesus that their brother was sick. It is a critical point to make that the message was not "Lazarus is sick," but, *"Lord, behold, he whom you love is sick"* (John 11:3). Jesus decided to not go see Lazarus immediately, but stayed where He was for two more days. Then, Jesus decided to go to Judea, a place where there was animosity against Him. Even though Jesus (whose miracles were well-known and whose word was always true) told them that Lazarus would not die, that his sickness would not result in death, the numerous accusations by the townspeople continued . These words likely impacted each disciple.

I imagine there was much discussion among the disciples. "Why is He waiting to see Lazarus?" "Judea? Is that a wise choice? Let's pray about it and ask God." (Well, maybe they didn't say that). Thomas made a most telling comment when they departed to go to Judea. "Then Thomas, who is called the Twin, said to his fellow disciples, 'Let us also go, that we may die with Him'"(John 11:16). Now, that's an encouraging send off. I suppose the name "doubting Thomas" was appropriate for this reason.

The two days passed and Jesus went to Bethany. It had now been four days since Lazarus died and was laid in the tomb. Upon His arrival, He noticed a crowd of people, in the house of Mary and Martha, comforting them regarding Lazarus. When Martha heard that Jesus had arrived, she left the house to meet Him. Or rather, she was "up and on the move," ready to confront the Son of God. Is it surprising that Martha heads toward Jesus, wanting a discussion, while Mary sits still in the house (John 11:20)? Remember, it was Mary who sat at the feet of Jesus, listening contemplatively, while Martha was active, busying herself with work. Again, we see the character of the two women as Martha wanted to engage Jesus in conversation. Her statement was respectful, showing a degree of former faith, yet lacking in active faith. *"Now Martha said to Jesus, 'Lord, if You had been here, my brother would not have died'"* (John 11:21). Martha knew Jesus could have saved Lazarus (former faith). She had seen and heard of many of His miracles. It was for this reason they sent word to Jesus and asked for a healing for their brother. Yet fear had robbed her of active faith. This is faith which can be called upon in the present. When all seems bleak, when there is no visual substance to believe, it is our active faith which wells up within us and awaits the touch from God. *"Now faith is the substance of things hoped for, the evidence of things not seen"* (Heb. 11:1). If she had still had faith, she would have asked God to speak forth words of life. It was Jesus who spoke the words, *"Your brother will rise again"* (John 11:23). Martha's lack of faith was again blatantly obvious in her words. She did not speak acknowledgment as to the possibility of a miracle, but instead, noted that Lazarus would rise, like all dead people, in the day of resurrection.

Mary and Martha had been pressured by the words of those around them. Instead of having a clear vision about the possibilities in God, they were discouraged and walked in a fear of the truth. They resigned themselves to the death of Lazarus, even though "the resurrection and the life"(John 11:25) stood in front of them. Did they not understand the healing power of Jesus? They had faith in the ability of God to heal their brother of sickness, yet were unable to extend that faith for a resurrection of their brother. Is God to be so limited by us? When we begin to place limitations on the power of God, we enter into a "wilderness" mentality. Remember the Hebrew people and the countless miracles of God which they witnessed. Plagues were sent upon the Egyptians to open up the opportunity for them to be free. The Red Sea parted so they could pass through and then, as suddenly as it parted, it closed upon their enemies. And still, the Israelites continually placed limitations upon God. "We don't have enough food, we are going to die." "We are thirsty, we are going to die." "We are surrounded by our enemies, we are going to die." They limited God in His authority and power in their life. They had a "wilderness" mentality.

How do people who know of God's divine power place barriers and restrictions upon Him? Mary and Martha were not able to seize upon their active faith because they had been polluted by discouragement and confusion. This blindness to the ability of Christ to heal their brother, to raise him from the dead was mainly due to—FEAR. Their minds must have been racing, hearing every comment made by the unbelieving crowd. "See, I told you He wouldn't come." "He wasn't really your friend." "Why did He wait before coming here? He doesn't care about us." And then, when Jesus did arrive, Martha acted in a way contrary to her belief system. She made a negative confession, one which displayed the true condition of her heart...one lacking faith. She had become confused, hurt, bewildered and fearful.

In this story, we have an excellent example of how to combat fear. Jesus did not argue, debate or fight with Martha. He simply told her the truth. He reiterated the truth *"Your brother will rise again"* (John 11:23), *"...He who believes in Me, though he may die, he shall live"* (John 11:25), *"And whoever lives and believes in Me shall never die..."* (John 11:26). Jesus concluded by asking Martha a poignant, straightforward question, *"Do you believe this?"* (John 11:26). The direct, honest way which Jesus approached Martha brought clarity to her. She was able to see through the fear and realize the significance of what she had been saying. Martha tells Jesus that she knows He is the Christ, the Son of the living God, who has come to the world (John 11:27). Once the truth is recognized and confessed, the cloud of confusion and fear is lifted off a person. Truth may come from a friend, a relative or a word from God (the Bible, prayer, prophecy). However, it may also come from the very person who placed the fear in you, the very source of the anxiety and defilement. Let me share a personal example.

A Personal Example

I had made a change in my teaching status and had moved to a different building, teaching at a different grade level. I was very excited about this change and was anxious for God to use me in this area. The first week of school passed; I met many of the teachers and was feeling very much a part of the staff. At the end of the first week, I had an encounter which influenced me for the rest of the year. One conversation, one quick dialogue and I became "trapped" for the next nine months. Fear is an odd emotion. It can come upon us so quickly, so suddenly. Before we even have a chance to respond, fear begins to wrap its tentacles around our heart and mind.

I was walking down the hallway, on my way to lunch, and I passed by Chris. She was a teacher in her mid-thirties whom I had met briefly in a meeting. I smiled at her and said, "Hello Cathy." She looked seriously at me and corrected me regarding her name. I sheepishly apologized, attributing my mistake to my being new and meeting so many new people. I casually commented about the number of students in the hallway and how crowded it was to walk. She returned my comments with a *stern, steady scowl*. My $30,000 education and my counseling credentials helped me immediately discern that something was amiss. Or perhaps, it was the hole that was now in my head as her icy glare numbed my forehead. Regardless, I knew we were not connecting very well and fear began to approach. I asked her if I had said something wrong. Her response only assisted fear to get a tighter grip on my mind. "Why would you care?" she said. "It's not like you would change." She retreated into her classroom, as the bell rang, signaling the beginning of the next period.

I gulped, took a deep breath (actually a shallow breath because I felt like someone was choking me) and followed her into her classroom. I wasn't sure what to say, but I knew something needed to be done. I had no desire of going through the rest of the day or week with someone upset with me. "Chris, could we meet after school to talk? I'm sorry if I have offended you." There was a bit of pleading in my voice.

Again, a withdrawn, distant response came forth, "It would be a waste of time. Your arrogance would get in the way." With that, she turned her back and the conversation was over.

Dejected and in shock, I walked down the hallway won-

dering how to respond. My mind was confused as I replayed the conversation over and over. What *had* I said? Was she right? Right about what? It didn't make any sense to me. And worse yet, her room was on the same floor as mine. I passed by her room several times a day. Was it too late to change jobs? There had to be an opening, perhaps, in some foreign country, for a fearful, defeated educator.

Within minutes, another teacher tracked me down. She asked how I was doing. I suppose having my lower lip drag on the floor was a slight indication that something wasn't right. This teacher explained that she had been in the hallway and had heard the whole conversation. I shook my head and had few words to offer in reply. The teacher told me to not take it personally as Chris had done this to many other teachers, especially men. She had several bad experiences in past relationships and was very bitter. From the consoling teacher's perspective, Chris was an angry person who often responded to people with venom and rage. Over the next thirty minutes, I had two other teachers approach me in an attempt to encourage and comfort me.

As the school day ended, I could not shake the heaviness upon me. I went to the principal, in an effort to obtain counsel. When I sat down in his office, he said, "Sounds like you met Chris today." I smiled weakly as I realized that the story had spread throughout the school (the joy of gossip). I shared my perspective and asked if I should approach her again, apologize, and attempt to smooth over the situation. His counsel was to leave it alone, as he concurred with the other staff members regarding her anger. He shared that she was a fine teacher, but struggled with relationships with fellow staff members. I was told she was much "better" than she used to be with people. How comforting.

As the weeks passed I found clever ways to avoid Chris. I walked to the other end of the hallway to get wherever I was going, even if it was just on the other side of her doorway. If she came into the office, I walked out. When she was walking toward me, I reversed directions or ducked into the nearest room. This may sound childish, (because it was) but I was scared of another encounter with her. I felt handcuffed, unable to approach her to reconcile, yet bound by the curses she had leveled at me. I spent time in prayer, hoping to get a direction for working with her. It was the end of October, when I felt an inspiration to reach out again.

The student government of the school was selling candygrams, as a fund-raiser. I purchased a little pumpkin-shaped card and wrote a note to Chris.

Dear Chris,
I am sorry we got off on the wrong foot. If I have been insensitive, please forgive me. I hope you have a great day and I look forward to working with you this coming year.

Sincerely,
Mike Sedler

The cards were given out on Halloween, but I did not receive any response. Throughout the year, there were numerous occasions where I found myself in the copy room, in the office or walking down the hallway and there was Chris. Occasionally, she would be cordial and say hello. Other times, she would ignore me. Each time, my heart would begin to pound and I would look for an escape route. I never did reach out again to Chris. I was gripped by fear and was unwilling to place myself in a place of being "hurt" again.

The last week of school arrived. It was early morning before school and I was cleaning up my room for the upcoming summer break. I looked up and in my doorway was Chris. The windows were closed and locked, she was blocking the only doorway. I was terrified. I boldly looked up, straightened up my 5' 6" frame (I am sure I was an impressive sight) and said, "Hi." She asked if I had a moment to talk. My heart sank as the grip of fear came upon me. All I could think about was the encounter nine months earlier. My confidence was gone, no scriptures of strength were brought to mind. I let fear literally rob me of my faith, hope and confidence in God.

I answered Chris in the affirmative and asked her to come into the room. Her words were cautious, but purposeful. Her voice had a lightness to it, with a twinge of sadness. As I listened to her speak, the fear began to dissipate, being replaced with a compassion and love for a wounded sister. "Mike, I'm sorry," she began slowly. "Earlier in the year, I should not have said the things I did to you."

In my haste to make things better, I quickly interjected, "It's okay. I'm sorry if I was insensitive." She persisted,

"No, it wasn't you. It is me. I have a lot of issues that need to be taken care of in my life. I am moving out of the area and taking another job. I shouldn't have taken my frustration out on you. I appreciate your reaching out to me. I am sorry I couldn't respond. Please forgive me." My smile and words of forgiveness seemed to lift a weight off her shoulders. She shook my hand and walked away. As I shook my head in disbelief, the Lord began to reveal my sin.

I had allowed fear to come on me to such an extent that it had prevented me from praying for a hurting individual. My own emotions had paralyzed me. Instead of recognizing the opportunity to pour out God's love, I became frightened and distant. Fear had thrown such a blanket of confusion upon me that I was unwilling, not unable, to persist in an area of outreach to another person. I say "unwilling" because I know God's power and authority could easily have purged the fear from my thoughts, if I had allowed Him. *You are of God, little children, and have overcome them, because He who is in you is greater than he who is in the world* (1 John 4:4). Fear infected my opportunity to minister, to reach out and, perhaps, even to evangelize to another person. Chris should not have "attacked" me verbally, but it was my sin, the sin of holding onto fear, which prevented her from being healed that year. The one who spoke fear into my life was also the one who opened my eyes to the truth of God. I am so grateful for Chris and her willingness to speak to me the last week of the school year. She not only freed me from my fear, but she was a vehicle for God's teaching me a valuable lesson. I don't know where you are today, Chris, but if by some exciting design of God you are reading this book, I wish to write you one more note.

> Dear Chris,
> I am sorry I was not more sensitive to you and your situation. I know God has a love for you and a desire to see you healed of past hurts. I lift up a prayer for you and trust that God has brought others into your life to touch and heal your broken heart. May your life be full of joy.
> Sincerely,
> Mike Sedler

Earlier, in this chapter, I mentioned a counseling session. The couple had taken on the posture of negativity brought about by fear. Our approach to them was simple, yet purposeful. We modeled the approach which Jesus used with Martha. No, we didn't say that we were the "Resurrection and the Life." We did begin to speak the truth to the couple. We recounted the ways in which God had used them to minister to others. We reminded them that they had a calling on their lives. We discussed the words which had been spoken over them and had them share their dreams of life. As they began to share these areas of their lives, it was as if the veil or cloud was lifted from them. They began to weep and ask for forgiveness for their loss of hope. They spoke words of commitment to one another and words of healing.

Now, listen, they still had issues to deal with in their marriage. But, they are together today, working through their problems via counseling, accountability, prayer and support. Fear tries to negate the truth by overshadowing it with worry and false scenarios. **Speak truth to your fears**.

If you are in a situation where fear has robbed you of hope and dreams, take a moment to ask for God's clarity in your life. Do it now! If your marriage seems too broken to be fixed, your relationship with your children too cold to ever connect again, stop now and pray. Perhaps, as I did, you have let fear blind you to people and their hurts.

Ask God for forgiveness and direction. If you don't have the words, read the following prayer out loud and stand on the truth of God's word.

Dear Heavenly Father,

*It has been so hard to see the truth when my eyes have been on me. **My** fears, **my** hurts, **my** pain. Lord, I want my life to be free of fear, of terror and the paralysis it brings. I open myself up to you, God. Touch me with Your light, Your Spirit, Your warmth. I can't do this on my own. I have tried, and failed. Please touch my marriage, my children, and my friends... I rebuke the spirit of fear from my life. It will not direct me nor will it corrupt me. I am free from that sense of terror and its choking oppression. I refuse to succumb to the negativity it brings and receive God's hope and destiny in my life. Thank you, O Lord, for hearing my prayer. I will continue to respond to Your word of life. Allow your word of truth in the Bible to speak to my heart. Let my words of worship and praise be a sweet aroma to you. I release Your Holy Spirit to cleanse me. I love You, Lord. Amen.*

QUESTIONS—Examining the Heart

1. Do you remember a time when fear was gripping your decisions and your perspective? How did you handle it? Is it still a problem? If so, read the above prayer again.

2. Like Martha, do you ever have faith in God, only to have it stripped away by situations? Make a list of areas in which you allow fear to come into your life. Share this list with another brother/sister and begin to pray against those open areas.

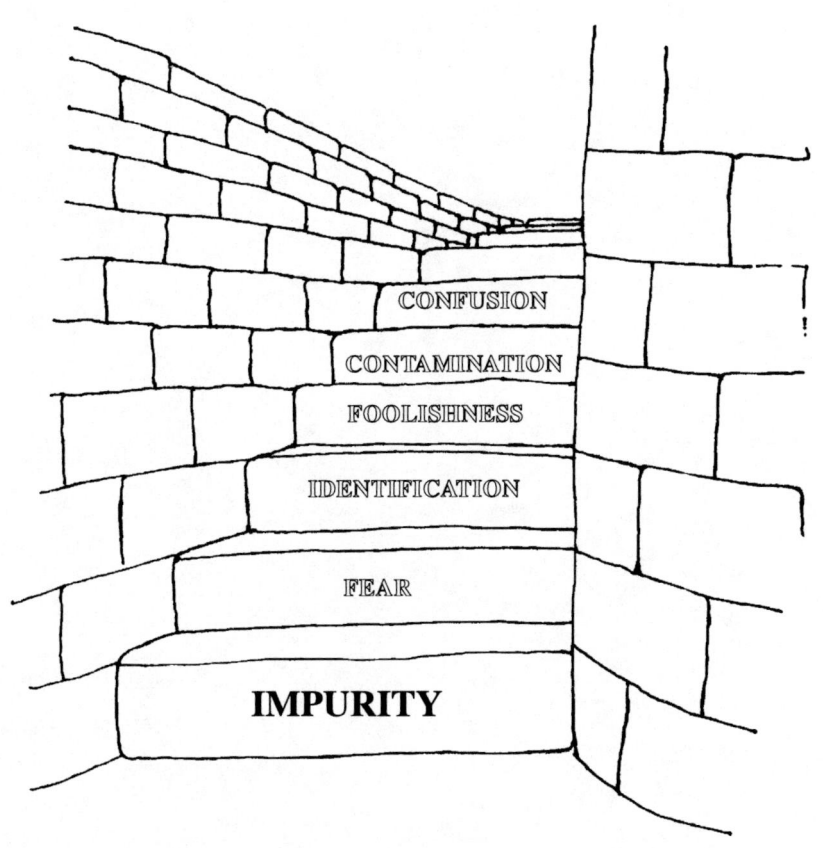

CHAPTER 9

IMPURITY

In this section, we will explore the depth of the impact of an evil report upon the listener. While a few of the previous stairsteps may seem somewhat subtle in regard to their impact on a life, even appearing minor in nature, the sixth stairstep, called **impurity**, is far from subtle. It manifests itself through contact with other people and will violently impact a spirit and life. Each word uttered by an impure person is like a dripping poison. The nature of the impurity creates fear, paralysis, false impressions of other people and eventually leads one into the deadliest of snares, **deception.** (It will be discussed in the next chapter). Let us examine what it looks like and how it impacts people.

> **IMPURITY:** One receives an evil report from a person, takes it into their spirit and, even though contrary to other information already known, believes it to be true.

A Jewish Perspective

During the 1930s and 1940s, a man by the name of Adolph Hitler used the spirit of impurity to defile an entire nation and pollute millions of people. His approach was simple, but diabolical. He mesmerized the people into believing that he had a plan, a direction, which would lead them to a better life. This included pointing out those people (Jews, elderly, handicapped, homosexuals, etc...) who would interfere with this plan and how they would create a barrier to the future of Germany. It was a slow, subtle seduction of the people. His oratorical skills, charismatic gestures and convincing concepts blinded the morals of many people. Impurity, while violent in its nature, is very crafty in implementation. Initially, Hitler was not very popular among the people. He was seen as emotionally unstable, extreme in his ideology and in his approaches. The people continued to listen, even though they may not have agreed. In time, confusion set in, then contamination and each stairstep pulled the people deeper toward deception. Slowly, cleverly and artfully, Hitler polluted a nation with impure words and deeds.

He surrounded himself with others with similar beliefs and convictions (as Absalom did in Israel). There were many who were unsure what they believed, but they followed the crowd. The Nuremberg War Trials brought legal conviction to many of the guards and officers in the concentration death camps for being a part of the killing of thousands and millions of people. The most common defense of these soldiers was, "I was just following orders." To many of us, this grotesque and hideous occurrence is inconceivable. How could anyone be a part of these atrocities? Where was their conscience, their sense of morality? For some, I can tell you where these areas were in their lives. Impurity blinded the people of their "common sense." All of their understanding was poisoned, tainted, contaminated and desecrated. Individual thought had given way to group priorities. And, the group priority was directed by a man who was bitter, contaminated and polluted with hatred and self-exaltation.

I grew up in a Jewish home. I had my Bar-Mitzvah at the age of thirteen and went through my confirmation classes at the age of sixteen. The majority of my friends were Jewish and the bulk of my social life surrounded Jewish activities. I was part of a youth group which met at the Jewish Community Center, and regularly attended the functions. We had city-wide gatherings, dances and sporting events. Each year, we had a state-wide youth event, where we had special speakers and an inspirational focus. All this was geared toward encouraging our Jewish faith and way of life. I remember one year, a Rabbi from another city shared about the prejudice and hatred toward the Jewish people. He gave us an historical perspective of the persecution of the Jewish people. There was an emphasis on the lies which were spread in early history and which increased during the years of the Roman Empire. He spoke of the deception of Gentiles (non-Jews) and how their hatred for the Jews infiltrated the cultures of the world. The Jewish people were blamed for the death of Christ and this bias created the death of many Jews in the past 2,000 years.

When I left that weekend, I realized that being Jewish could create a separation from others in my life. Suddenly, each comment and conversation that carried any hint of anti-Semitism was magnified in my life. Comments like, "I jewed him down," which meant, "I talked him down to a lower price," seemed rampant in my school. The ignorance of these expressions only solidified my growing segregation from non-Jews. In an ominous way, it seemed that there was a general disdain for Jewish people. I noticed that people were jealous of financial success or educational accomplishments of Jewish families. It was during this year of my life that my awareness exploded through two powerful encounters. The first event occurred when I saw a fight at my school that started when a boy called another "a dirty Jew." It was the first time I had seen prejudice directed toward me (or my culture and religion). Suddenly, the racism projected toward people of color or culture became more vivid in my mind. Not long after this event, we had a history teacher who hung a Nazi flag in his room, as we studied Germany and World War II. This blatant act of insensitivity was disturbing to many of my friends, as well as myself. To study the historical facts of a war was one thing, but to display a flag representing an army that killed over six million Jewish people was an insult. One young girl in my school burst into tears as she recalled the story of her grandparents being killed in the "showers without water" by the Nazi regime. It seemed the more I looked, the more I saw. A few years later, during the 1972 Olympics, Israeli athletes were killed, for being Jewish. My concern and confusion only deepened during this season of my life.

When I went to college, this confusion was amplified. I left Phoenix and went to a college in San Diego, CA. I was surrounded by strangers, without my support systems. My loving parents were not around me nor were my high school friends. Again, the prejudice was blatant, without hesitation. I kept my religious beliefs to myself for the first months, cautious as to the response from my fellow classmates. However, as time progressed, I began to explore the attitudes of those around me. My personal confidence and pride in being Jewish allowed me to be more assertive. "Why would you call a Jewish person a cheapskate?" I asked. "What do you mean, 'you jewed him down'?" I challenged. In time, it was apparent to me that most people had no idea what they were talking about. They had been raised in homes which spoke these phrases and they had become a part of their own vocabulary. The impurity which surrounded them had shaped their own personal viewpoints. I began to see some of these people with a new understanding, almost one of pity. They had allowed a polluted and foolish spirit to control their perspective.

As I looked back upon my own life, I saw how this was true for me also. I thought of people from Germany as killers and murderers. It was unfathomable to me how anyone could allow the death of six million Jewish people to occur without raising a hand. You see, I had never heard of Corrie ten Boom, Dietrich Bonhoeffer or the countless others who had stood for godliness during this heinous time. Like those around me, I had allowed my own inward perception to create a fog-like mentality toward other people.

Impurity clouds one's perspective on life. We begin to only see and hear from those who appear confident, sure and right. Dissenting voices are viewed as weaklings and said to be shortsighted. Our own convictions become secondary as we begin to get caught up in the charisma of the moment. The synergy* of emotions can overwhelm

---

*Synergy occurs when separate components begin to operate together, and cooperatively, thus creating an infusion of corporate energy greater than the individual energy available.

us, to such an extent, we begin to question our own beliefs and attitudes. This isn't necessarily bad, if we pursue truth and honestly engage in a mission to strengthen personal belief systems. It was through one of these times of searching for truth and the challenges to my own perspectives which allowed me to hear of the reality of Jesus Christ. At the age of twenty-two, God revealed the truth of Christ's dying for my sins and His resurrection life. For over 20 years, I have walked in a confidence and freedom that is only found through the grace of God. I am grateful to God's loving hand extending toward me during many times of my life.

Impurity can drive us closer to God, cause us to seek out truth and clarity in life. Or it can bring about a terrible confusion and devastation. When impurity touches us, a quick decision must be made to avoid a spreading of defilement in a life. If one embraces the thoughts, even momentarily, confusion will follow. It doesn't take much time for a person to become defiled by impure thoughts and actions. The entertaining of a lustful thought can open up a door for pornography or adultery.

A casual statement which stretches the truth allows us to begin to embellish a story and ultimately lie. By merely "touching" things which are defiling, we can become polluted. It was for this reason, God commanded the Jewish people to stay away from animals or people who were dead. *"Whoever touches the body of anyone who has died, and does not purify himself, defiles the tabernacle of the Lord"* (Lev. 19:13). *"Whatever the unclean person touches shall be unclean..."* (Lev. 19:22). Disease and stench are passed on from dead things. Death can only bring death, unless we allow the life of Christ to touch us.

A problem occurs when we think we are right and therefore don't need to respond. We might think, "Truth will eventually come out and people will see the error of their way." Due to this mentality, we usually sit back and let natural events occur in life. In Germany, this is what happened. The majority of the people may not have liked what was going on, but the paralysis of impurity prevented most people from responding. "There is nothing we can do" "If we just stay quiet, they will leave us alone" "Things will get better, eventually." I have uttered every one of those statements in my life. They are powerless, impotent thoughts which allow us to be open to mindless control by those with impurity in their spirit. When impurity touches us, we begin to say and do things which we normally might not do, but the violent contact of impurity confounds our thinking. The Bible relates an incident that exemplifies this chaotic mind set.

The Impurity of Shimei

After Absalom's treason against his father, we read that David escaped from Jerusalem. He must have been discouraged, even feeling guilty for his son's turning against him. In his travels, King David was confronted by Ziba, who gave an evil report about Mephibosheth. This must have compounded David's sense of frustration and, perhaps, depression. I can hear David saying, "Lord, what else can go wrong today?"

What else, indeed? David rode a little further and was confronted by Shimei, the son of Gera, who lived in the house of Saul. Imagine the number of negative comments Shimei must have heard toward David. Having lived around Saul most of his life, Shimei must have been contaminated and polluted, over and over again.

The following description of the incident is almost beyond belief. It is a ludicrous description of a crazed man, totally infected with impurity.

> ...He (Shimei) came out, cursing continuously as he came. And he threw stones at David and at all the servants of King David. And all the people and all the mighty men were on his right hand and on his left. Also Shimei said thus when he cursed: "Come out! Come out! You bloodthirsty man, you rogue! The Lord has brought upon you all the blood of the house of Saul, in whose place you have reigned; and the Lord has delivered the kingdom into the hand of Absalom your son. So now you are caught in your own evil, because you are a bloodthirsty man"
>
> 2 Sam. 16: 5-8

Please, take a minute and picture this scene. A raging man came out and began to curse the king and threw rocks at him. As if that were not enough, he challenged him and called him worthless. At the same time, David was surrounded by all the people **and his mighty men**. Excuse my common language, but what kind of an idiot would do such a thing? I'll tell you what kind—one who is so wrought with impurity that he is not thinking of consequences or in a rational frame of mind. Even though the words being spoken were Shimei's, I imagine the "spirit of Saul" was quite evident.

I love the response of Abishai, one of David's men, *"Why should this dead dog curse my lord the king? Please, let me go over and take off his head"* (2 Sam. 16:9). David told his men to leave Shimei alone. He felt that if Absalom, his own son, hated him, how much more could someone not of his flesh hate him? This response by King David could be more a reflection of his discouragement rather than wanting to show mercy to an enemy. He even commented, *"It may be that the Lord will look on my affliction, and that the Lord will repay me with good for his cursing this day"* (2 Sam. 16:12).

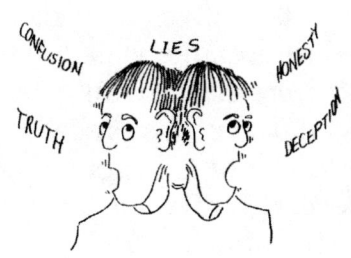

Here we read about a man of God (David), with a powerful army at his disposal, but his own sense of confusion (from Saul's and Absalom's attacks) rendered him unable to respond in a godly manner. At the same time, we see how impurity placed an individual (Shimei) in a precarious position, one which ultimately led to his death (read 1 Kings 2).

Impurity occurs when we hear evil reports with our natural ears and mind without seeking for spiritual wisdom and understanding. If we accept the words of others as truth, we will become filled with a mixture of philosophies, attitudes and beliefs. *"Don't be stupid and believe all you hear; be smart and know where you are headed"* (Prov. 14:15, CEV). If we listen to an evil report, we will become so filled with wrong attitudes, conclusions and actions, we will defile everything we touch. There are several characteristics of the impurity stage. They will help you define whether the stairstep of impurity has set into one's life.

CHARACTERISTICS OF IMPURITY

1. Trusting and believing the evil report is accurate. It is crucial to protect our spirits from hearing and receiving an evil report. Our tendency may be to believe the report due to past experiences or situations, but this will only open up the door to further impurity. *"An evildoer gives heed to false lips..."* (Prov. 17:4). Do not be one who runs *to* evil, be one who runs *from* evil. I believe the story of Ananias and Sapphira, found in Acts 5, gives us a clear picture of how to avoid an evil report. Ananias stated that he and his wife sold land and they were giving it all to the Lord. It was a lie, as they kept back part of the proceeds. Ananias was struck dead by the Spirit of God for lying (not for withholding money). Several hours later, Peter had Sapphira come and share with him. Peter did not assume, by the reports of Ananias, that she was guilty of deception. The Bible tells us that Peter asked her whether the amount given to the church was an accurate account of the sale. She had every opportunity to repent, be honest, explain or clarify. Instead, she too lied and suffered the same fate as her husband. Peter, following a very godly approach, did not listen to the report of Ananias, knowing he was a liar. Peter checked it out for himself instead of passing judgment on Sapphira. As it turned out, Sapphira's words condemned her.

2. Forming negative **opinions** based on the report. This is a symptom of one who is infected with impurity. Our thoughts become skewed toward an individual, our memory distorts occurrences and we begin to feel and think negatively toward the individual. It doesn't matter whether we are personally involved in the situation, an observer or in a third party discussion.

In high school, I associated with many different groups of

people. There were two particular individuals, Gary and Cal, who were very good friends of mine. However, they did not like one another and, therefore, the three of us seldom did things together. Their lack of appreciation for one another stemmed from their older brothers. A specific area of competitiveness had been placed within them by their brothers. In all that Cal and Gary attempted, their older brothers would compare them, boast of their exploits or set up a situation of competition. Gary and Cal formed opinions about one another, without even getting to know one another. I would hear one of them say something totally erroneous about the other, but not knowing how to handle it, I would laugh or ignore it. There were times I found myself impacted by the distorted reports shared by one friend or the other. Obviously, this caused a breach in my friendship with one or the other. The offense becomes ours, we personalize it and it is as if we were directly a part of the situation. *"It is impossible that no offenses should come, but woe to him through whom they do come"*(Luke 17:1)!

Acts 5 tells the story of Peter and the other apostles being brought before the high priest and a council of elders. Many accusations were directed toward the men of God. In the midst of the council, a man stood up by the name of Gamaliel. His guidance to the elders was very clear. He told them that if what the apostles were saying was of men, it would fade away. But, if it was God, the council was setting themselves against an undefeatable foe. Gamaliel was saying to the people, "Don't pick up an offense. If God is a part of this and you set yourself up against Him, look out!" We must ask ourselves whether we are picking up an offense due to the attitudes of other people. Guard your ears and your heart from such deceptions.

3. Viewing an individual in a distorted perspective. Often times, when we believe an evil report to be true, we no longer see a person the same way. We don't trust them, don't enjoy their company, and feel they are superficial and judgmental. The areas which we once appreciated about them are no longer visible, overshadowed by our twisted thinking and contaminated spirit. This can be deadly in a church setting. Where once, the pastor or elder was seen as a man or woman of God, it is difficult to receive from them. I was recently talking to a member of our church and this person shared that it was difficult to receive from one of the elders in the church. As I explored this area, it was clear that this person had an offense against this elder. The situation which was used as the foundation for the offense had been misunderstood and was inaccurate in its translation. (I had first hand knowledge of the truth of the matter). My counsel was for the person to go to the elder and ask for further elucidation in the matter. I believed this would lead to clarity and a probable repentance on the part of the individual.

4. Failure to discern and question the motives of the potential false witness. A key "test" as to whether impurity has overtaken us rests in this area. Do we interpret the reporter's words as "supporting evidence" of an infraction or do we weigh the motives? Proverbs 16:2 speaks to the core of this issue—"*All the ways of a man are pure in his own eyes, But the Lord weighs the spirits* (or motives)." When we naively assume people will be caring, honest and compassionate, we overlook the basis of the Gospel. We are sinners and are apt to lie and deceive for our own benefit. Remember what the Bible says about the heart. "*The heart is deceitful above all things. And desperately wicked...*" (Jer. 17:9). "*Truly the hearts of the sons of men are full of evil; madness is in their hearts while they live...*" (Eccl. 9:3). Our tendencies are to see the negative in people, to be hurt, offended and bitter.

I know of people who share their marriage difficulties with their parent(s) or siblings. This eventually causes these people to have bitter feelings toward the (in-law) spouse. I have seen many marriages destroyed because a person has foolishly contaminated relatives against his or her spouse. The results are devastating and create a barrier to reconciliation or unity within a marriage. Think about it for a minute. If I am struggling in my marriage and tell my relatives (dad, mom, brothers, etc.) about the issues, their tendency will be to side with me, their own flesh and blood. As this continues, their perspective will be distorted and their view of my wife will be negative. Even if things get better, it will be difficult to change the "family" perception of her.

If a person comes to you with a negative report, the first reaction should not be to believe it, but to look at their motivation. Why would I complain about my spouse unless I was frustrated, angry or hurt? Are people usually thinking clearly and objectively when they are in these emotional states? This leads to negative reports, distortion of facts and a sense of wanting an ally for complaints. In fact, the stronger the person speaks the false report, the more I look at their spirit. *"There is a way that seems right to a man, But its end is the way of death"* (Prov. 16:25).

5. Withdrawing from a person, especially in the spirit. Impurity creates a desire to distance ourselves from people. We may say we feel uncomfortable with them or don't enjoy their company. The reality is we have become impure and taken up an offense. I have noticed this within the framework of the church. If someone is upset at another person, they limit their contact with the person. I have seen people who are upset with a pastor, so they don't go forward for prayer or ask for spiritual support. I have seen pastors walk around people because they have held onto an evil report about a person. (Embarrassingly, I admit that I have been one of those ministers.) And likewise, I have seen people in the congregation avoid a pastor for the same reason. This is a clear sign of impurity, one which needs immediate repentance and cleansing from the Holy Spirit.

In Acts 9:13, we read the story of Saul of Tarsus (Paul) coming to Ananias for prayer. The Lord prepared Ananias for the coming of Saul, but Ananias shared his fear of having Saul show up. *"Then Ananias answered, 'Lord, I have heard from many about this man, how much harm he has done to Your saints in Jerusalem. And here he has authority from the chief priests to bind all who call on Your name."* Clearly, the reports Ananias had heard were true, but the situation had now changed. Because he listened to reports about Saul, Ananias was led to respond in impurity. Fortunately, he was able to hear the clear word of God and receive correction. Are you able to hear the clear voice of God, one which can bring clarification and truth to an impure situation?

6. Repeating the false report to others (being a false witness). Naturally, if we feel justified in our emotions to withdraw, think evil of others and believe evil to be truth, it is not a large step to move into gossip and murmuring. Once we allow impurity to rule our lives, we become a vessel for evil reports. Like a magnet, we attract others and they are drawn to us. It doesn't take too long before we are so confused that good looks bad and bad looks good.

We are now one step away from deception. It may seem

like a long, hard road to get there, but it happens so quickly. A person who was once so excited about God can become spiritually "dead" in a moment of time, if he or she allows defilement into their life. Notice what happens the next time you wash your car. You may drive it away from the car wash or, after washing it in the driveway, you drive it a block or two and dirt settles on the car. Every bird in the area recognizes the shine and glare of clean chrome as a target of defilement. Even the clouds understand that a "washed car" means it is time to rain. When God washes us clean, we now become a greater target for the devil. Putting on the armor of God (Eph. 6) is essential for a strong walk in the faith. If you are one who has allowed impurity to rule your life, get clean (repent), and put on the armor of God—truth, righteousness, peace, faith, salvation, prayer—against these, an evil report cannot prosper or grow. We have climbed six stairsteps. This leads us to the culmination of a defiled spirit—the pitfall called "deception."

QUESTIONS—Examining the Heart

1. Why do you think people hear an evil report without questioning the motives?

2. Look at the "Characteristics of Impurity" again. Have you ever followed this progression in your life?

3. When you are discouraged from the "spiritual warfare" of life, do you put on the armor of God? If not, commit to doing this and see the difference.

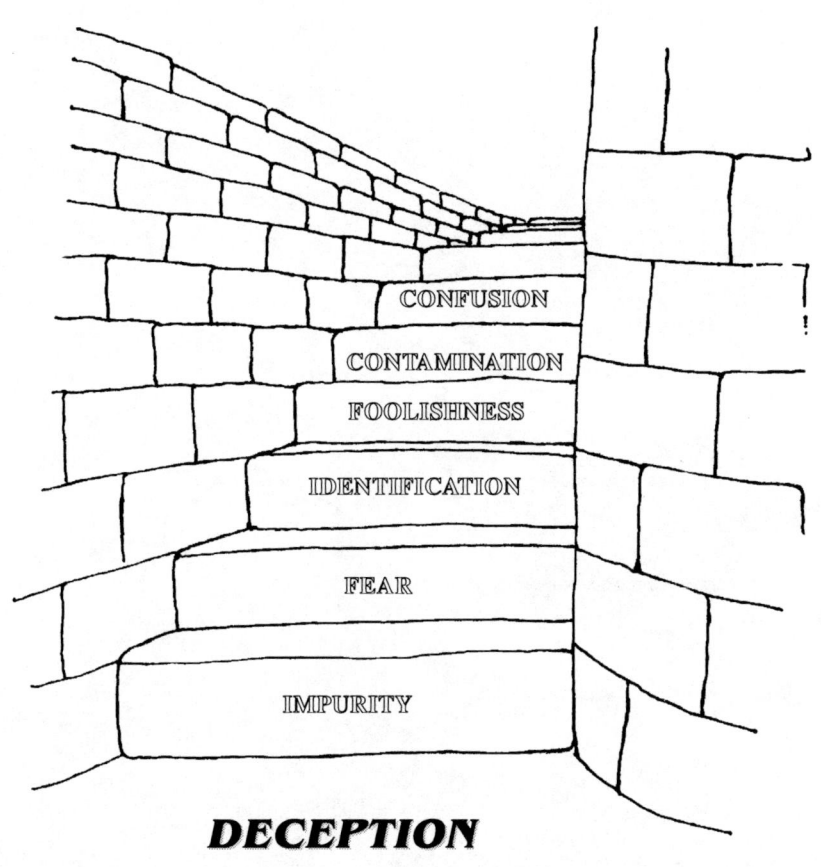

CHAPTER 10

DECEPTION

Deception is a place of impurity, adulteration and corruption of spirit. Deception may allow one to be a pawn in the hands of the person who defiled them. The deceitfulness of the evil report corrupts our spirits and taints our perspective on people and life. Deception is so deadly that it literally leads to the breaking of relationships and covenant in marriage, church, families and among friends. The Christian community is wrought with this disease and its impact upon the church is devastating. Until a church is willing to confront the sin of gossip and evil reporting, there will be constant divisions and factions separating people from one another and from leadership.

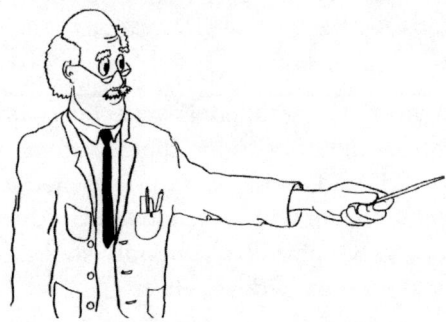

DECEPTION: Being misled by what is false and refusing to listen to, investigate, or receive the truth.

Of course, this problem is so rampant that it is well beyond the walls of the church. The business community, schools, homes and neighborhoods are easy prey for the deceived individual. When we repeat negative reports or situations, we separate people from one another. This creates a precipice in a relationship—dangerous terrain—which may not be easily negotiated by the people involved. The Bible outlines the consequences for spreading rumors among people:

- *"...He who repeats a matter separates friends"* (Prov. 17:9).
- *"Whoever guards his mouth and tongue keeps his soul from troubles"* (Prov. 21:23).
- *"A false witness will not go unpunished, and he who speaks lies shall perish"* (Prov. 19:9).

One who is pulled into the area of deception is manipulated by the very essence of the evil report. They have connected with the one who gave them the evil report and have thus established an ungodly "soul tie"* that will impact them emotionally, mentally, physically and spiritually. This ungodly relationship creates a cycle and pattern of sin which grieves God and the Holy Spirit. The person who is in deception becomes a slave to the evil report and perpetuates it by taking up an offense and then spreading rumors and stories with increased tenacity. There are several symptoms of the deceived person, which we will discuss in this chapter. As these are pre-

---

* The term "soul tie" refers to a spiritual or emotional connection with an individual. This may be godly or ungodly. In the Bible, Ruth and Naomi had a godly soul tie, as did David and Jonathan. These led to spiritual blessings and a closer relationship with God. However, Ahab and Jezebel along with Ananias and Sapphira had ungodly soul ties which led to deception, deceit and ultimately destruction.

sented, keep an open mind and an open spirit so God can reveal truths to you and confront areas of deception in your own life.

Many years ago, a family in the church I attend became dissatisfied with their involvement and role within the church. This dissatisfaction grew into a grumbling about the services, the music, the pastors, the youth group, etc. It is interesting, though, that when these people became upset, even minor, unrelated problems became magnified. (I have seen this in marriages, in parent-child relationships and among friends.) What had been a minor issue, became the focal point of the situation. While the frustration of the family was real and needed to be discussed and resolved, the parents took it upon themselves to gain as many allies as possible. This took the form of phone calls to other people, having people over to their house and then sharing grievances against others, and writing letters of persuasion to key individuals.

These people used their position of influence and their friendships in an attempt to alienate people from the church, from leaders, from God and to justify their own beliefs and attitudes. They brought defilement upon other people and passed their disease of offense to as many as would receive it. While it was difficult to see these people spread their words of poison, it was even more devastating to watch other people soak it up. Fortunately, the majority of those exposed to this tactic rejected it and confronted the people for their sin of defilement.

Deception can be clear and easy to spot, *if* you are not the one directly involved in the deception. A little six-year-old boy once said to me after he had been around someone wrought with deception, "What's wrong with him?

He seems really mad at everybody." Even a child could sense and see the problems in this person's life. In this chapter, I will carefully explain ways to recognize deception. If, while reading this chapter, you find yourself defensive or emotionally stirred, stop and ask God if there is any deception or defilement working within you. The intent of this chapter is to expose deception and help each one of us to grasp the godly principles of purity and restoration.

Signs of Deception

SIGN # 1—*An individual receives another's offense (or false report) and uses it as an excuse for their own rebellion.* This lack of maturity and honesty within one's life leads to further justification regarding their behavior. Eventually, decisions will be made which have serious spiritual and natural ramifications. This occurs frequently among groups of friends or acquaintances. An individual becomes upset with someone, targets them and shares their frustration with their social group. Then, those with a tendency toward rebellion, pick up on this offense and deception follows. It is not uncommon for this group to "encourage" or "support" further areas of antagonism toward the selected target. Leaders, pastors, supervisors —pay attention! This type of action may also occur from those with influence and can create tremendous damage and hurt within businesses, a home, a church or an organization. The one in charge often carries tremendous responsibility and authority. If he or she shares a negative report to the general population, those with unguarded spirits will become contaminated, thus perpetuating the defilement.

In the Book of Esther, Haman was asked by Queen Esther to come to a banquet. Unbeknownst to Haman, Esther was going to use the meal as an opportunity to expose his plan of destruction against the Jewish people. However, he thought the banquet was going to be used to honor him and to shower him with accolades.

> *So Haman went out that day joyful and with a glad heart; but when Haman saw Mordecai in the king's gate, and that he did not stand or tremble before him, he was filled with indignation against Mordecai.*
>
> Esther 5:9

When Haman went home, he gathered his wife and friends and told them of the honor of being asked to this banquet. He also shared his anger and frustration with Mordecai. In fact, he stated emphatically that even though a great honor was being given to him, it was of no significance because of the impetuousness and dishonoring of Mordecai, the Jew.

Haman's wife and friends wanted to please him, to revel in his glory, perhaps even to receive some of his upcoming riches. Their own rebellious, dishonest hearts became exposed.

> *Then his wife Zeresh and all his friends said to him, "Let a gallows be made, fifty cubits high, and in the morning suggest to the king that Mordecai be hanged on it; then go merrily with the king to the banquet." And the thing pleased Haman; so he had the gallows made.*
>
> Esther 5:14

The pattern is so clear and is often repeated. An evil report is given, people take in the offense and become defiled. In turn, in their own deception, they become a part of the murmuring and gossip. As in the case of Haman, his so-called "friends" added fuel to the fire of defilement.

When the time of the banquet arrived, Queen Esther told the king of Haman's plan. The unveiling of his true intentions led Haman to try to lie, to disguise the fact that he wanted to kill the Jewish people. The story of Haman ends with his being hung on the very gallows he had built for Mordecai. What Satan so often intends as evil, God turns toward the good of His people.

Joseph's brothers sold him into slavery, yet God established Joseph as an authority in Egypt. Joseph's testimony, despite his being a slave, unjustly imprisoned and torn away from his family, is one of victory. In speaking to his brothers, Joseph stated, *"But as for you, you meant evil against me; but God meant it for good..."* (Gen. 50:20). There are consequences and repercussions for impurity, defilement, lies and deception. These occur in both the natural and spiritual realm. Do not allow yourself to become deceived by taking on another person's offense or complaint.

SIGN # 2—*Actively seeking out false or evil reports about people*. It may appear that this person is like a news reporter, interviewing and questioning others in an effort to garner negative information about a person or situation. Or perhaps a better illustration is that of an archeologist digging up old artifacts and bones, trying to piece together occurrences from the past. *"An ungodly man digs up evil, and it is on his lips like a burning fire"* (Prov. 16:27). Beware of this type of person as they will surely influence you and create confusion in your life. The picture they paint seems very real and accurate, yet underneath, the canvas is one of deception and dishonesty.

The Pharisees and the religious people were chronically attempting to "dig" up information to be used against Jesus.

> *Now it happened, as Jesus sat at the table in the house, that behold, many tax collectors and sinners came and sat down with Him and His disciples. And when the Pharisees saw it, they said to His disciples, "Why does your Teacher eat with tax collectors and sinners?"*
>
> Matt. 9:10, 11
>
> *And when the Pharisees saw it (the disciples eating in the grainfield on the Sabbath), they said to Him, "Look, Your disciples are doing what is not lawful to do on the Sabbath!"*
>
> Matt 12:2
>
> *And behold, there was a man who had a withered hand. And they asked Him, saying "Is it lawful to heal on the Sabbath?"—that they might accuse Him...Then the Pharisees went out and plotted against Him, how they might destroy Him*
>
> Matt. 12:10, 14

Those in deception must continually attempt to justify their stance and belief. It seems, if they stop and truly examine what is occurring around them, they must admit their faults and their wrong perspective. Unable, or incapable because of their unrepentant heart, the individual continues a life of deception and defilement.

SIGN # 3—*Seeking out others to agree with us.* This was discussed earlier as we studied the life of Absalom. Through rationalization and manipulation, Absalom was able to justify his own usurpation of authority from King David. There is tremendous strength and power when we join forces, in agreement with other people. This is what Korah did to Moses, what Absalom did to David, and what the religious people did to Jesus. Another powerful example is seen in the Book of Acts. We read about a group of Jewish people who joined together to kill the apostle Paul.

> *And when it was day, some of the Jews banded together and bound themselves under an oath, saying that they would neither eat nor drink till they had killed Paul. Now there were more than forty who had formed this conspiracy.*
>
> Acts 23:12, 13

We have heard it said, "There is safety in numbers." This is the essence of the person in deception. The more people they can rally to their side, the more confident they become.

A Fresh Revelation

Have you ever had the experience of reading the Bible and, although you have read a certain passage many times, suddenly the words bring fresh revelation to you? Recently this happened to me. I was reading in Judges about Gideon. It was as if God had replaced my Bible with a new one and had inserted new passages in it. I began to read about Abimelech and the depth of deception in his life. I saw things I had never noticed before and they brought a new conviction in my life to stay pure from deception. Let me recount the incidents surrounding Abimelech's life.

Gideon (also called Jerubbaal) had seventy sons from numerous wives. In addition, through his relationship with a concubine from Shechem, he bore a son named Abimelech. Upon Gideon's death, the people of Israel turned away from God, began to worship idols and came against Gideon's family. Abimelech went to Shechem and spoke to his uncles and the rest of her family.

> *"Please speak in the hearing of all the men of Shechem: 'Which is better for you, that all seventy of the sons of Gideon reign over you, or that one reign over you?' Remember that I am your own flesh and bone."*
>
> Judg. 9:2

Basically, Abimelech is saying "Look, why not let me be the ruler over you? At least we are immediate family. These other people are not as 'close' as we are and there are seventy of them. Each one would be over you. Choose me and it will be better." The family responded to Abimelech's plea and gave him money. This money was used to hire assassins.

> *...Abimelech hired worthless and reckless men; and they followed him. Then he went to his father's house at Ophrah and killed his brothers, the seventy sons of Gideon, on one stone. But Jotham the youngest was left, because he hid himself.*
>
> Judg. 9:4-5

The people of Shechem gathered and made Abimelech their king and he reigned over Israel for three years. However, as usually happens with situations that are birthed out of sin and corruption, it turned sour on

Abimelech. God sent a spirit of division between Abimelech and the people of Shechem and *"the men of Shechem dealt treacherously with Abimelech"* (Judg. 9:23). It is typical that people turn against one another when their relationship has no depth and is only built on self-exaltation or a common hatred or jealousy toward others. It is at this point, we find a common thread throughout the aforementioned situations of Absalom, Korah and Abimelech. You know the saying, "What goes around, comes around?" We are about to see the reality of this statement.

The people of Shechem desired to have Abimelech killed and set people to ambush him throughout the mountains. There was one individual, whose name was Gaal, whom the people of Shechem looked to for guidance.

> *Then Gaal the son of Ebed said, "Who is Abimelech, and who is Shechem, that we should serve him? Is he not the son of Jerubbaal, and is not Zebul his officer? Serve the men of Hamor the father of Shechem; but why should we serve him? If only this people were under my authority! Then I would remove Abimelech."*
>
> Judg. 9:28, 29

Does this sound familiar? "If only I were king!" "If only I were in charge!" "If only you entrusted the power to me!" The power of deception infiltrates a person's mind and actions, but the strength of it is multiplied by gaining support of other people.

Abimelech spent the next period of his life fighting and running for his life. The end of his life came while he was trying to burn down the castle tower of an enemy. While standing at the door of the tower, a woman pushed a millstone from the top of the wall and it landed on Abimelech's head. He was severely wounded and, to avoid dying a slow, painful death, he had one of his soldiers stab him. He did not want to be remembered as the man who had a stone pushed on his head, but rather as one who died in battle by a sword. However, since his story has been captured historically by the Bible, it would appear his attempt to cover up the "falling rock" story was a failure.

SIGN # 4—*Believing we are doing the will of God by coming against one another.* A position of self-righteousness, an arrogance clouds the mind and we justify our attacks toward others by seeing their faults and sins. We may feel that we are God's instrument of judgment or vengeance. This is very dangerous as one may begin to feel they are above moral law, ethical law or even God's law. As discussed earlier, King Saul felt he was able to carry out his own agenda by modifying the directions of God (1 Sam. 13 and 15). Saul's life was full of contradictions and deceptions. He spent many years of his life trying to kill the one (David) who had been anointed by God to succeed him on the throne. In contrast to King Saul and his blatant efforts to come against David are the more typical, sometimes subtle behaviors, which many of us use in life. A negative word toward a co-worker, a false story about a peer or "friend," the evil report about leadership, these are the ways of deception.

Questionable Motives

In the late 1970s, I worked as a counselor at a state correctional facility for juveniles. There were children from ages ten to eighteen in the facility. They were incarcerated for a minimum of nine months and up to two and a half years. This was a secure facility, with locks on the doors, a constant security patrol around the perimeter of the buildings and each employee carried a walkie-talkie strapped to his side. Occasionally, a resident would try to escape by hitting a counselor over the head with a broom, pulling a kitchen knife on them or by simply wandering away from the group outside.

One of the counselors, Joan, had been there for many years. She was a seasoned veteran who the residents did not mess around with very much. She had applied for numerous supervisory positions, but had not been promoted. This had caused an offense to build up within her which manifested itself through negative talk about the supervisors, a "better" way to do things and a covert stirring of insurrection among the residents. Joan would tell a resident that he was being treated too harshly and that she would talk to the supervisor about it. She would approach the employees with changes which needed to take place and ask for their support in the upcoming staff meetings. Joan was the champion of the residents and the mouthpiece for the staff. She worked in the same cottage which I did, and we frequently worked together. Joan knew I was a Christian, and we would talk about "spiritual matters" from time to time. It was also not uncommon for her to speak of God and prayer.

I had been working at the juvenile center for about five months when an incident occurred that, as I look back upon it, demonstrated the pattern of deception. Joan had always been friendly and caring toward me. She helped me through orientation and would frequently "guide me" in my daily activities. Personally, as a 23-year-old young adult, I appreciated her concern and input, as my experiences were limited.

As the months passed, I also became friends with one of the other counselors, Martin, and with our supervisor, Pat. We played basketball and worked out together. Unfortunately, Joan was upset with both Martin and Pat. She was jealous of Pat's supervisory status and of Martin's close relationship with Pat. As time went on, Joan began to make negative comments to me about Pat. She began to question decisions he made and suggested "alternative" solutions. ("If only I were the supervisor!") When I was paired with Martin on a day shift, she would warn me of possible problems that might develop when one worked with him. In time, I began to eye these two with some leeriness and hesitancy. One day, Pat and I were playing football with the residents on the outside courtyard. While it was suggested that we never leave the cottage totally empty, the day was beautiful, all the residents were with us, and I was with my supervisor. We enjoyed a game of football for about thirty to forty-five minutes and then did our daily chores in the cottage.

When I arrived at work the next day, I was summoned to the office of Dr. Ransly, the superintendent of the facility. I had *never* been in his office and was quite nervous about being summoned to meet with him. As I walked into his office, my heart sank. Not only was the superintendent in the office, but Sherry, the case manager of the facility, and a sheepish-looking Pat were present in this meeting. Dr. Ransly began to share how important it was to follow all the rules of the facility. His words were something like, "Mike, with over 200 adolescents in this facility, it is important for all of us to follow the same rules. Would you agree?" My affirmative response did little to change the stern, serious look on his face. What was this all about? What rules? Why were we all in this office? Questions raced through my mind, but I said nothing.

Dr. Ransly, with the help of Sherry, laid out the scenario for which I was being disciplined. It was at this point, that the proverbial light bulb went on. You see, Joan had tried to call the cottage the day before when we were playing football. If it had been an emergency, she could have had the operator, or security, contact us on our radios. She did contact security, and they informed her we were outside, playing football. (We didn't find this out until a week or so later, when one of the security officers told Pat.) At this point, she called the superintendent's office and, in a very concerned voice, said she was desperately trying to get a hold of the cottage and there was no answer. She couldn't understand this as the *"rules"* were very clear and Pat, the supervisor, was supposed to be in the cottage all day. As Pat arrived the next day, there was the note from Dr. Ransly, and he began to investigate. 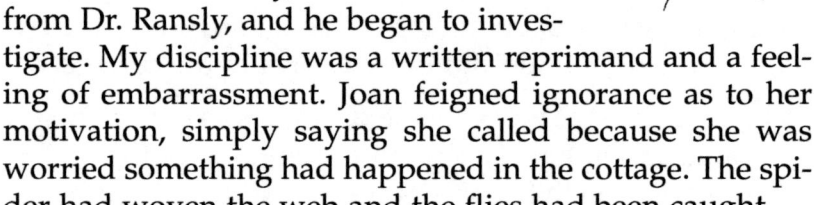 My discipline was a written reprimand and a feeling of embarrassment. Joan feigned ignorance as to her motivation, simply saying she called because she was worried something had happened in the cottage. The spider had woven the web and the flies had been caught.

As I recall this incident, Joan's motivation and intentions seem very clear. Joan had been injured by rejection in her personal and professional life. Though she had a place of responsibility and recognition, she wanted more. It was not enough for her to be the senior counselor, she coveted more. I was caught in the middle, attached to an individual (Pat) who had been targeted by her plans. Over the next months, Joan's depth of impurity and deception became evident. She withdrew from people and openly stirred up strife among the residents and counselors. Eventually, she was transferred to another cottage. Her refusal to look at her own life and to actively pursue truth created a barrier in all her relationships. Her new assignment lasted only a short time and she soon left. Her willingness to help me and give me guidance appeared genuine, yet was actually a part of her need to control and groom me for her own support and advancement. She wanted people to agree with her, not grow with her.

People who operate in deception may be helpful, caring and pleasant to be around when everything is going their way in life. But, if a person disagrees or the situation takes a turn contrary to their desires, the sheep turns into a wolf quickly. One who is in deception frequently blames others for the problems in life, the difficulties in circumstances.

The Bible recounts an incident where Elijah, a recognized prophet in the land, was going to see King Ahab. Elijah had already proclaimed a drought upon the land, as a judgment from the Lord, and the king was obviously a bit miffed by this occurrence. Instead of King Ahab's repenting and finding out what needed to change in order for rain to fall upon the land, he looked for a scapegoat. Deception creates an attitude of blame, a pointing of fingers toward other people.

> ...and Ahab went to meet Elijah. Then it happened, when Ahab saw Elijah, that Ahab said to him, "Is that you, O troubler of Israel?" And he answered, "I have not troubled Israel, but you and your father's house have, in that you have forsaken the commandments of the Lord and have followed the Baals."
> 1 Kings 18:16-18

In an attempt to shift blame from himself, Ahab readily accused Elijah of being the "trouble of Israel." The person in deception does not receive counsel, correction or guidance. They quickly look for the nearest scapegoat and focus as much blame in that direction as possible.

I believe we have all had the experience of being verbally attacked and assaulted by another individual. This is especially difficult when the attack comes from a brother or sister in Christ. Psalm 55 speaks of the hurt caused by friends who turn against us.

> *For it is not an enemy who reproaches; then I could bear it. Nor is it one who hates me who has exalted himself against me; Then I could hide from him. But it was you, a man my equal, My companion and my acquaintance. We took sweet counsel together, and walked to the house of God in the throng.*
>
> Psa. 55:12-14

David eloquently expressed his hurt and pain when a "friend" came against him. Harsh words from a friend or family member cut a much deeper wound than those of a stranger or someone who does not have intimate experiences or memories with us.

The subject of God's people coming against one another is of grave concern to many in the church community. The Bible speaks to this issue in both the Old and New Testament. God intended for us to follow a godly appeal process (Matt. 18) and not to bring a carnal judgment against one another through the courts system. When we, as children of God, use an ungodly institution to carry out our concerns, we allow unrighteousness to enter into the equation. I am not implying that the legal system should never be utilized. However, I do believe God desires us to work out our differences through a godly process and avoid taking our issues before the courts, if at all possible.

> *If then you have judgments concerning things pertaining to this life, do you appoint those who are least esteemed by the church to judge? I say this to your shame. Is it so, that there is not a wise man among you, not even one, who will be able to judge between his brethren? But brother goes to law against brother, and that before unbelievers! Now therefore, it is already an utter failure for you that you go to law against one another. Why do you not rather accept wrong? Why do you not rather let yourselves be cheated? No, you yourselves do wrong and cheat, and you do these things to your brethren! Do you not know that the unrighteous will not inherit the kingdom of God?* **Do not be deceived.**
>
> 1 Cor. 6: 4-9 (emphasis added)

In recent years, I have read about Christian leaders questioning the validity of a "move of God" in certain areas of the country or world. The attitude seems to be that if the Spirit of God is demonstrated in a way contrary to "my" belief system, "my" experiences or that of "my" church, it must be wrong. Entire church denominations refuse to fellowship with one another because of doctrinal differences. One church promotes contemporary music while another utilizes hymns. A church may lift their hands to God and dance in praise and worship. Another church has pews and sits quietly during worship and during the sermons, without an "amen" or "hallelujah" being uttered. Yet, all these differences can serve to separate us from one another instead of recognizing the broad spectrum within the family of God. I have actually heard the term "anti-Christ" used to describe a specific church and its leader. The poor testimony and witness of Christians against Christians and churches against churches has occurred in such epic proportions that many unbelievers use the word "hypocrite" to speak of the church world. Each group or individual feels they have heard from God and therefore are justified in their attacks and sharing of an evil report. Once again, we need to ask ourselves "Am I attempting to restore a person or to uncover a person?"

SIGN # 5—*Refusing to receive counsel because "everyone else is wrong."* If an individual becomes so confident in "self" that they refuse to listen to others, deception is upon them. *"Where there is no counsel, the people fall; But in the multitude of counselors there is safety"* (Prov. 11:14). One year ago, I was approached by a young woman who was planning to get married. Jenny had been married several times before, each time the relationship had ended in divorce, multiplying her emotional scars. She had several children, each one a product of a different marriage. Jenny was now planning on getting married again. As I met with her, it was evident she did not want my counsel or guidance, but she did want my blessing on her upcoming marriage. In talking with her, she admitted that a number of other people had discouraged her from going forth with this endeavor. I told Jenny that I agreed with the other's discernment and encouraged her to go through pre-marital counseling. She became upset and told me that I just didn't understand. She had "heard from God" and she was to get married.

Jenny got married the next week. Within a month, I received a call from Jenny and Carl (her new husband) for marriage counseling. The next few months were filled with phone calls and counseling appointments. Unfortunately, the foundation of the marriage was built on sandy ground. Despite numerous interventions, the marriage failed. Recently I sat down with Jenny and shared some strong, forthright words with her. In our time together, she agreed that her fleshly desires for a companion outweighed her spiritual reasoning. Although numerous friends had warned her about "jumping into" a new marriage prematurely, she did not heed their counsel. Another scar, another hurt had entered her life.

Jenny is not a bad person for choosing the direction she did in life. She desired something good (marriage), but was unwilling to prepare appropriately. Her selfish desires were placed above biblical counsel. People in deception will often say they have heard from God, but cannot explain why others have heard something different. It is an odd, but common, occurrence when a person refuses to listen to the people around them. Those giving counsel are usually friends, family, spiritual leaders or accountability partners. Suddenly, all these people "do not understand the situation." It is frightening when an individual thinks they are the only one who can hear from God. This isolationist mentality creates a tendency to withdraw from people. Decisions are then based on emotions rather than on the Spirit of God. *"The way of a fool is right in his own eyes, But he who heeds counsel is wise"* (Prov. 12:15).

SIGN # 6—*Isolating one's self from godly contacts with friends, family and leadership.* Think about it. Why would a person who is self-focused, self-centered or in rebellion want to be around people who are challenging them to seek God for guidance? When you see a person pulling back, refusing to fellowship with friends and family, isolating themselves from the Word of God, beware! This is a person who is walking on the road of deception.

> *To the pure all things are pure, but to those who are defiled and unbelieving nothing is pure; but even their mind and conscience are defiled. They profess to*

> *know God, but in works they deny Him, being abominable, disobedient, and disqualified for every good work.*
>
> Tit. 1:15, 16

Stephen is a young man in our church who, at one time, felt a deep love for God and the "family of God." In recent years, his time has been pulled toward his job and career. Understandably, if he was to be effective at his job and receive promotions, he needed to spend more time and energy in his job. As time went on, meetings, which had always been on non-church nights, spilled over and began to conflict with church. At first, it was only once a month, then twice, then...you know the story. Stephen no longer connected with his Christian friends because so much time was spent around his work.

Some of his friends tried to approach him and share what they saw as the beginning of an imbalance in his life. This concern was not well received. He poured more and more time into his career. Stephen used to read the Bible, pray and seek Christian relationship. He now finds other sources of relationship and connection. His most recent comment was, "I just don't have anything in common with the people in church." The sad part is that the decision Stephen is making affects his family and children. A decision to remove one's self from God's life giving presence impacts everyone around them. I still have hope and faith that Stephen will see what has become of his life. Unfortunately, his isolation and his refusal to interact with God's people, the very ones who could speak life to him, has been greatly reduced. *"A man who isolates himself seeks his own desire; He rages against all sound wisdom"* (Prov. 18:1).

Deception is a one-way ticket to spiritual death. Without

a Holy Ghost interruption in a life, deception, like a giant boa constrictor, will suffocate and squeeze the very life out of a person. They will feel the pressure, the spiritual life flowing out of them, but they will be so entrenched in the coils of deception, it will be easier to give up rather than fight. This is what happens to most people in deception. They argue, they attack, they become embittered and eventually grow weary and fall into a lifeless routine without any hope of change. A bleak and depressing picture? Yes, it is. But, without Jesus Christ being active in your life, what hope is there to escape the snare of deception?

QUESTIONS—Examining the Heart

1. Do any of the signs of deception show up in your life? If so, which ones?

2. If you have recognized any symptoms of deception creeping into the life of a friend or family member, how might you address the situation?

3. Are you keeping company with people who are in deception? Are their "companions" in your life who interfere with you accomplishing all of God's plan for your life?

THE CLEANSING PROCESS

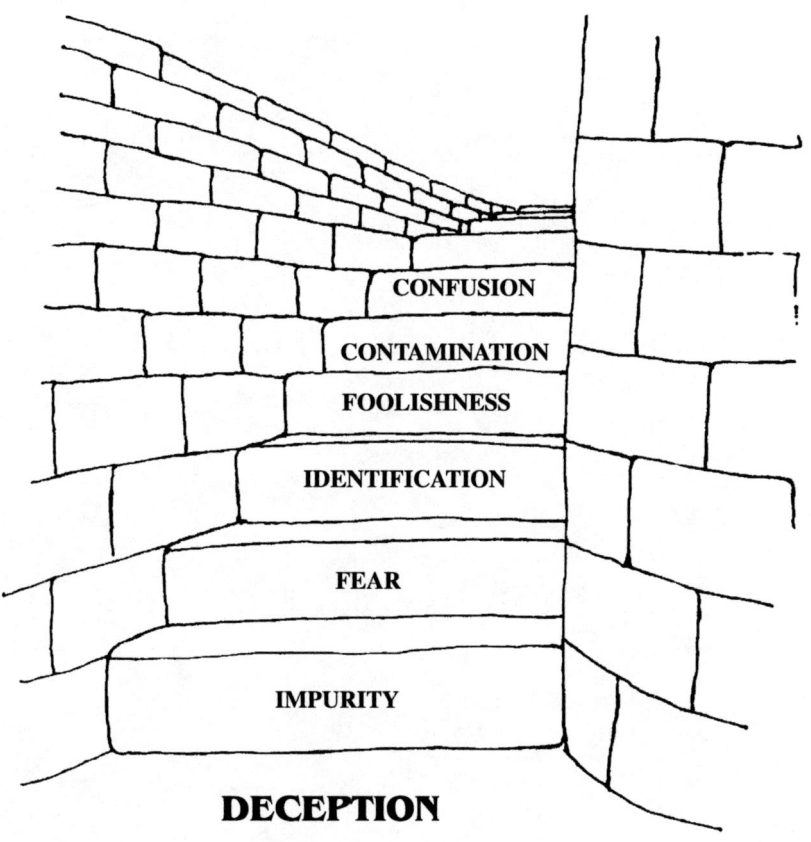

CHAPTER 11

THE CLEANSING PROCESS

Dear Lord,

So far today, God, I've done all right. I haven't gossiped, haven't lost my temper, haven't been greedy, grumpy, nasty, selfish or over-indulgent. I'm really glad about that.

But in a few minutes, God, I'm going to get out of bed and from then on, I'm probably going to need a lot more help.

Thank you, In Jesus Name,

Amen

So, let's get out of bed and get going with what God has for us today. For those who don't feel you can overcome some of the areas we have discussed in this book, you can stay in bed, pull the covers over your head and pretend to be asleep. Or, you can read this chapter and it will help you to understand the cleansing process of God when one is defiled by an evil report.

"I don't wanna get washed up. I'm not dirty. I didn't play with any germs." How many of us have heard this phrase from our children or said it when we were young? It is indeed amazing how my son can play basketball for so many hours, yet never get dirty. His insistence that "I didn't sweat" or that "I only touched the ball with my hands" is comical. Recently, I was in a store and the person next to me had a very pungent aroma. In watching others respond and react with a wrinkled up nose, a disgusted look on their face or even a look of disbelief, it became evident that this person did not realize he/she was giving off a sour smell. This is how deception affects us in life. We don't recognize the foul odor we are giving off or the filth upon our bodies.

Our perception can be dependent on other factors in our life. For example, if I finished mowing the lawn, but plan on continuing to work outside, I would not feel a need to get clean. However, if I were going to meet some friends at a movie, my tendency would be to get cleaned up (much to the relief of my friends). As long as I was going to be around "dirty" areas, why clean up? When I am in the midst of dirt and grime, I may not recognize how dirty I am at the time. A group of skunks may be very comfortable with the smell of one another, but include a cat in the group and at least one animal will be unhappy. How does this relate to the area of defilement?

Marty had a circle of co-workers who continued to speak negatively toward their supervisor. At first, it didn't seem like a big deal. He enjoyed work and liked his employer. But in time, Marty found that, he too, was frustrated with the supervisor's attitude and lack of compassion. Soon he noticed that she seldom came out of her office, except to complain and yell. Although Marty's wife had pointed out his change in attitude, he minimized the problem. (There are usually people attempting to warn us about becoming polluted, but our self-centered nature keeps us from hearing these people.) *"Whoever loves instruction loves knowledge, but he who hates correction is stupid"* (Prov. 12:1).

Marty needed to get "cleaned up" from the defiling conversation poured out by his fellow employees. What prevented Marty and others like him from becoming cleansed from the polluting lifestyle at his workplace? A major stumbling block was his decision to continue to engage his colleagues in negative conversation. If our perception is that we are only going to get dirty again or that we don't need to be clean for the next job we do, there is no motivation for purification. Unless Marty saw that his conversations with his co-workers kept him defiled, he would not desire a change. As long as the group was homogenous, the smell would never be identified. What they needed was for someone to stand up and proclaim the conversation "foul." They needed someone like you, an individual who understands the implications of listening to negative conversations. If even one person stands up and makes a statement for cleanliness in the conversation, this can drastically change the course of future discussions.

What allowed Marty to receive an evil report? What factors in his life or in his job left him susceptible to listening to false reports from others? Personal dissatisfaction, frustration and negative attitudes were but a few areas that Marty needed to explore in his life. As long as he continued to "wallow in the mud" there was no need to get cleaned up. *"When wisdom enters your heart, and knowledge is pleasant to your soul, discretion will preserve you; Understanding will keep you"* (Prov. 2:10,11).

Is becoming cleansed as easy as saying, "I'm dirty and want to be cleansed?" Let me give a definitive answer— "Yes *and* no." We can answer, "Yes," as God is able to come and purify us with a fresh breath from the Holy Spirit. However, we can say, "No," because any cleansing or healing must be walked out. Does an alcoholic person become clean by admitting she is an alcoholic **or** by staying sober? Does an adulterer become purified by admitting the sinful action **or** by true repentance, an act of turning the other way in 180-degree behavior? It is important to recognize our condition, our sin. Yet this recognition must be coupled with prayer, guidance, action, faith and direction.

Am I Leprous?

There was a man in the Old Testament who was defiled. He was dirty, smelly and impure. He couldn't run away from it nor could he become clean on his own. He admitted his impurity, yet each day it remained with him. No amount of hiding it, telling people about it, or denying it changed the fact that this man was impure, defiled, dirty and soon to become an outcast. However, a young stranger spoke a word of truth to this man. She told him of a way to become cleansed, a way which would take him down a path contrary to any he had been down before. He had a choice to make—whether to become bitter and offended at his lot in life or whether to pursue a difficult, cleansing process. Which path did he follow?

Let's read the story of Naaman, the leper.

Now Naaman, commander of the army of the king of Syria, was a great and honorable man in the eyes of his master, because by him the Lord had given victory to Syria. He was also a mighty man of valor, but a leper. And the Syrians had gone out on raids, and had brought back captive a young girl from the land of Israel. She waited on Naaman's wife. Then she said to her mistress, "If only my master were with the prophet who is in Samaria! For he would heal him of his leprosy." And Naaman went in and told his master, saying, "Thus and thus said the girl who is from the land of Israel." Then the king of Syria said, "Go now, and I will send a letter to the king of Israel." So he departed and took with him ten talents of silver, six thousand shekels of gold, and ten changes of clothing. Then he brought the letter to the king of Israel, which said, 'Now be advised, when this letter comes to you, that I have sent Naaman my servant to you, that you may heal him of his leprosy.

And it happened, when the king of Israel read the letter, that he tore his clothes and said, "Am I God, to kill and make alive, that this man sends a man to me to heal him of his leprosy? Therefore please consider, and see how he seeks a quarrel with me." So it was, when Elisha the man of God heard that the king of Israel had torn his clothes, that he sent to the king, saying, "Why have you torn your clothes? Please let him come to me, and he shall know that there is a prophet in Israel." Then Naaman went with his horses and chariot, and he stood at the door of Elisha's house. And Elisha sent a messenger to him, saying, "Go and wash in the Jordan seven times, and your flesh shall be restored to you, and you shall be clean." But Naaman became furious and went away and said, "Indeed," I said to myself, "He will surely come out to me, and stand and call on the name of the Lord his God, and wave his hand over the place, and heal the leprosy."

"Are not the Abanah and the Pharpar, the rivers of Damascus better than all the waters of Israel? Could I not wash in them and be clean?" So he turned and went away in a rage. And his servants came near and spoke to him, and said, "My father, if the prophet had told you to do something great, would you not have done it? How much more then, when he says to you, 'Wash, and be clean'?" So he went down and dipped seven times in the Jordan, according to the saying of the man of God; and his flesh was restored like the flesh of a little child, and he was clean. And he returned to the man of God, he and all his aides, and came and stood before him; and he said, "Indeed, now I know that there is no God in all the earth, except in Israel; now therefore, please take a gift from your servant." But he said, "As the Lord lives, before whom I stand, I will receive nothing." And he urged him to take, but he refused. So Naaman said, "Then, if not, please let your servant be given two mule loads of earth; for your servant will no longer offer either burnt offerings or sacrifice to other gods, but to the Lord. Yet in this thing may the Lord pardon your servant when my master goes into the temple of Rimmon to worship there, and he leans on my hand, and I bow down in the temple of Rimmon—when I bow down in the temple of Rimmon, may the Lord please pardon your servant in this thing."

2 Kings 5:1-18

I believe Naaman expressed in the natural how we should become cleansed in the spiritual. He is a godly example of one who was defiled (in the natural) and needed to be cleansed. There were many obstacles to this cleansing (distance, finances, communication, anger, pride and disillusionment, to name a few). Does this list look familiar? It is the very same list that prevented others (Judas, Absalom, King Saul...) from achieving their cleansing.

Attempts to bring restoration to an individual who has fallen into sin or deception will usually be unsuccessful unless one addresses the area of being polluted by an evil report. Once this is addressed, repented of and prayed for, then the Holy Spirit can bring forgiveness, love, humility, understanding and guidance to the person. I know *this* seems like a strong statement, but if you have read this book carefully and let the Spirit of Christ minister to you, there is a witness to this process.

> *To the pure all things are pure, but to those who are defiled and unbelieving nothing is pure; but even their mind and conscience are defiled. They profess to know God, but in works they deny Him, being abominable, disobedient, and disqualified for every good work.*
>
> Tit. 1:15, 16

Now *that* was a strong statement! Let's examine, step by step, what Naaman did to obtain his healing and cleansing in life.

Apprehending a Cleansing for Your Life

1. Naaman recognized his condition. Now, you might be saying, "Of course Naaman recognized his condition, it was so obvious. His skin was flaky, his nose and ears swollen and his arms were a mass of sores and scabs. My sin is very minor and no one can notice my condition, it is easy to hide." Well, I wonder. It is so common to think our problems are small, insignificant, unnoticed. The reality is that people can see our defilement; they can smell it; they hear it; they touch and taste it. The real question is not, "Do other people see my defilement?" but "Do I see my own defilement?" How long had Naaman been leprous? How long had he been hiding it under his armor, his clothing? Was he so defiled that he was unable to be intimate with his wife and family? Did his peers and his servants whisper, "Unclean, unclean," when he walked among them? How much longer would it have been before Naaman's skin would rot away completely, before his nose or his ear might fall off?

The servant girl spoke a word to Naaman's wife who shared it with Naaman. Together, in unity, they took a hold of the word and confronted his leprosy. What other choice did he have? You see, when we are the "living dead" what future do we have? If you are leprous with gossip, offense and hurt, you are rotting away spiritually. As Naaman did, confront your sin and admit your condition of defilement. This is the first step toward cleansing.

2. Naaman had a desire to be cleansed. In verse 4, we read that Naaman approached his master regarding his situation. Naaman, being a man under authority, understood the importance of going to his master. He recognized the necessity of approaching a higher power and authority with his situation. When we are feeling overwhelmed, confronted by a problem beyond our comprehension, do we approach our authority and higher power Jesus Christ?

Remember the story of the centurion? The Book of Luke tells this account of the man whose servant was ill. This centurion did not request for Jesus to come to his home and pray for his servant. His faith was so great that he knew that a word from the Master, the authority, would heal his servant. He approached Jesus, stating, *"Therefore I did not even think myself worthy to come to You. But say the word, and my servant will be healed. For I also am a man under authority..."* (Luke 7:7, 8). Can each of us say to God, "For I also am a man (or woman) under authority?" Let's take a *little* **test**, a *small* **quiz** on authority. Do you speak negatively about your supervisor (boss, parents, teachers, church leaders)? Would your "authorities" in life see you as under authority or against authority? When was the last time you blessed your authorities, spoke encouraging words to them or supported them in an open forum?

Simply having a desire for something is not enough. If Naaman had only had a desire, but no understanding of authority, he would have left on his own, no kingly letter in his hand, and walked boldly, even brazenly into the court of the king of Israel. Minimally, Naaman would have been laughed out of Israel, but most likely, Naaman would have been killed for dishonoring and insulting the king for his presumptuous attitude toward being cleansed. There are usually many obstacles and confrontations to achieving a cleansing in a life. If desire alone is not enough, what else does one need to receive a total cleansing from God?

3. Naaman would not be distracted from receiving his cleansing. Have you ever mapped out a plan in your mind, known exactly how it should occur, what was to be said and how you would respond? Yes, it was a great plan, but one small problem occurred. It didn't happen the way you thought it should. Unfulfilled expectation can create disappointment and hurt feelings.

Recently, Joyce and I planned to go out for the evening. All day we talked about how nice the dinner was going to be and how enjoyable it would be to just relax and talk to one another. Right before we were leaving, a phone call came from a couple in our church. Their son had been in an accident and was at the hospital. The couple was shaken by the incident as the doctors were talking about the need for emergency surgery. For the next hour or two, I encouraged and prayed with this couple at the hospital. When I returned home, it was too late to go out. Our "beautiful dream" evening was over. The next couple of hours were not very pleasant in our home. Both of us were grumpy and impatient with each other. As the evening neared an end, we began talking and realized that our frustration was neither at each other nor at the couple who had called. It was a disappointment in not having our intended plans that evening fulfilled. Our image of the night was shattered leaving frustration and unfulfilled dreams.

Naaman was confronted with this type of calamity in his life. He surmised that all he had to do was take a letter to the king and he would receive a healing. But, in verse seven, we find that the king was far from excited to see Naaman. In fact, he was angry, believing Naaman was trying to provoke a war by embarrassing the king. The king tore his clothes, as a sign of mourning, and believed that Naaman had been sent for an ulterior, military motive. The king rejected Naaman's plea for help and probably had him removed from his presence. It was at this point that Naaman could have been sidetracked, offended or discouraged.

This was the critical time for Naaman. Would he return home, defeated and downcast? Would he leave Israel speaking evil of the king for his refusal to help a commander from a neighboring land? Naaman stood at a crossroads in his life. What would you have done? How do you respond when you don't get your way? Do you become disillusioned or discouraged with a situation or person? Do you (or I) allow God to direct our words and our course of action? We often fall into traps (or habit patterns) which prevent us from hearing God's voice. Until we break these patterns, our cleansing will be delayed and, probably be temporary in length.

Elisha heard that the king had torn his robes and volunteered to intercede in the matter. In fact, Elisha told the king that Naaman should come see him so that *"he shall know that there is a prophet in Israel"* (2 Kings 5:8). What boldness and confidence Elisha had in God. This was not an arrogant man saying, "I can do it!" This was a humble servant who knew what his God could do in the life of a submitted man. So the message went forth for Naaman.

I have often wondered how long it took for the message to get to the king. Think about it. How long after the king tore his clothes did Elisha find out about it? An hour? A day? A week? Then Elisha responded to the situation with a message to the king. Another day? Two days? Or more? Remember, there were no quick phone calls. Elisha could not be contacted via a web-site or e-mail address such as *www.prophet.com*.

This information transaction could have

taken days or even weeks. The Bible does not tell us the time frame of this communication, but I believe it is a significant point to ponder. Naaman, hurt, wounded, rejected, disappointed, was still in the area. He hadn't left to go "home" and wallow in self-pity. No, Naaman wanted a miracle and was bound and determined to apprehend his cleansing. He must have been waiting—waiting for the right direction, guidance and purpose. He knew what he wanted and would **not** be distracted.

A Problem Arises
(or "Satan Baits Naaman, Again")

> *And Elisha sent a messenger to him, saying, "Go and wash in the Jordan seven times, and your flesh shall be restored to you, and you shall be clean."*
>
> 2 Kings 5:10

Have you ever seen the sign in someone's office which says, "What part of the word NO don't you understand"? This next section of scripture reminds me of this phrase. To me, the instructions were plain and clear. "Go wash in the Jordan seven times and you will be cleansed." After all those years of being leprous, of being embarrassed and afraid to have people touch you, Naaman was "seven dips" away from being restored to purity.

The Hebrew word for *clean* in this passage is *taher*. The Strong's Concordance shows this word to mean, "sound, clear, unadulterated, uncontaminated, innocent and pure, self-cleansing and purging." Elisha was offering Naaman a new start. We aren't talking about a "taking our car through the car wash" cleansing, but a "new paint job and super buff shine" cleansing. And all he had to do was follow the instructions of the prophet of God. Did it sound too easy, too simple? Did Naaman expect more from Elisha? As we read verse 10, we see that Naaman didn't even meet with Elisha, but with Elisha's messenger. Could Naaman have been offended that he did not get a personal audience with Elisha? Was Naaman upset that he was asked to bathe in the waters of the filthy Jordan River—waters that could not even compare to the clear quality of rivers in his home area? By now, how had Naaman built up his cleansing in his own mind? What was it supposed to look like? How was it supposed to occur? What would be the response of his wife, his friends, the king?

It seems that Naaman expected more than what he got from Elisha. Perhaps he had heard about the scene on Mt. Carmel with Elijah, Elisha's teacher and the prophets of Baal. Did Naaman expect lightening, trumpets and a pronouncement of his healing? Or maybe, Naaman started having doubts and fears about whether it could really happen to him? Many times, I find people who have tremendous faith for others, have a difficult time having faith for their own miracles. "I know God can heal their marriage, but I don't know about mine." "Yes, I believe God has financial provision for people, but as for me..." Isn't it usually easier to believe for others than for ourselves? Could Naaman have begun to doubt God's intervention into his life? Fortunately, Naaman was not distracted and still desirous of a cleansing.

4. Naaman was willing to receive counsel, correction and direction from others. This great, honorable man who was commander of the king of Syria's army was angry. The word used for his anger means to "burst out in rage" (v.11). Yet, in the midst of his frustration and anger, Naaman was willing to hear the voice of others. This is a key point in the cleansing process. Most likely, there will be multiple obstacles and barriers to your cleansing process. Why? If we are defiled and dirty, what kind of testimony are we to those in the world? However, once cleansed, we become a target for every demonic force of Satan. *"...your enemy, the devil, is like a roaring lion, sneaking around to find someone to attack"* (1 Pet. 5:8, CEV).

It is very difficult to "have ears that hear" at this point in the process. First of all, we don't see ourselves as defiled or polluted. We think we are right and can handle everything ourselves. The counsel given by other people is seen with suspicion. Often times, the motives of those giving counsel are seen as questionable. The person fighting the process of cleanliness uses words such as *manipulation, self-centered* and *control*. They see others as not understanding what they are going through, even accusing their closest friends and supporters of being insensitive and uncaring. Where a person was once able to challenge and guide a brother or sister in God, each comment or suggestion is now met with disdain and animosity. It is during this phase that people have a tendency to quit the process of cleanliness. In walking away from purity, these people blame and curse others for their lack of support and love.

When Naaman began to walk the path toward cleansing, he was confronted by a king who tried to pick a fight. Struggling with rejection and discouragement, Naaman's spirit was lifted by a message from Elisha. Soon, his soaring spirit was dashed by the prospect that Elisha would not meet with him. In his hurt state, Naaman may have thought this was due to the fact he was not worthy of an audience with the prophet of God. With this offense brewing in his soul, a final crushing blow was about to be delivered. Naaman was asked to do a simple, menial procedure, one that he easily could have completed in his hometown, under much "cleaner" circumstances. In his own mind, Naaman must have had many "better ideas" than washing in the river. People, circumstances, our own thoughts and situations, many which are demonically influenced, will oppose our process of cleansing. Satan does not want us to be clean, but **God does** want us to be pure and clean. *"...In the world you will have tribulation; but be of good cheer, I have overcome the world"* (John 16:33). Naaman confronted his flesh, his doubts and his anger and pursued cleansing. What a tremendous model of perseverance and determination he is to all of us. Naaman passed the test. He overcame the obstacles. He was now ready to take a final step of faith, one that would lead him to a brand new life.

5. Naaman was obedient and submitted to a higher authority. It can be very difficult to respond to a situation when one, personally, has a different perspective. In a recent staff meeting with the leadership of our church, I expressed a viewpoint that was in the minority. In fact, it was such a minority viewpoint that I was the only one who agreed with it. This should have been my first clue that perhaps, I needed to rethink and pray about it. (Oh, do I hear a witness?) However, being the "open-minded" person I can be at times, I thought everyone else simply needed more enlightenment. I had acted on impulse in a situation, without getting counsel, and my fellow pastors were asking me to explain the motivation behind my actions. The more I talked, the more confusing the situation became. I found myself feeling isolated, defensive and somewhat frustrated that my fellow ministers didn't "get it."

As the conversation continued, the Lord began to speak

to me regarding my pride and independence. At this point, I repented and asked forgiveness from the staff for my independent attitudes. The problem did not lie in the area of my different opinion, it was the way I expressed those opinions and my not giving credence to the other thoughts being expressed. Our senior pastor, Steve Allen, gently, but firmly helped me with an attitude adjustment when he spoke of my failure to obtain counsel and confirmation from others. Admittingly, this was difficult for my pride and ego. I don't like to make mistakes (who does?) and I especially don't like seeing the fleshly spirit of independence in my life.

In the days to come, my wife and I talked about the situation. Joyce frequently asked me if I was offended, or if I felt isolated, hurt or rejected. We openly challenge one another in this area to prevent the enemy from obtaining a foothold. Through a running dialogue with my wife and a fellow pastor at church, God was able to show me the tendency I have to react to situations. When I think I have an answer or direction, I will move toward a resolution or action in that arena. This can create an independent, isolating spirit that gives the impression that I don't need people and my "own competence" is sufficient to go it alone. Over the years of our marriage, Joyce needs to remind me of communicating and being a "team player" in our marriage.

The staff at our church are incredible. Each pastor and their spouse has a strong anointing of God. Many times, I have been spared from making errors in judgment by one of my fellow brothers or sisters, by their speaking a word of caution or discernment to me. Yet, there I was, in the midst of pulling back and making decisions without input from other members of the team. Imagine a basketball player running one play while the other players move into a conflicting offensive series. The confusion would be evident. This is why I needed to communicate with the other people. It was not that *what* I wanted to do was wrong or inappropriate, it was the *way* I did it. I was fighting the battle alone, without covering or protection. I had a big target on my back, the cross hairs of the enemy were upon me, and no one was around to warn me.

In the Bible, we find a discussion on unity and diversity addressing this issue (1 Cor. 12:12-27). I know I need the church family and all their gifts, but expediency (or is it foolishness?) can prove to be a downfall for me. Once I move into the mindset that God has only spoken truth to me, the enemy has set me up for failure. My tendency is to seclude myself from others' input that opens up the door for self-righteousness, arrogance and conceit to rule my spirit. It is only a matter of time before I fall into the pit of deception. This pattern needs to be broken in my life. I am thankful that I have accountability with other people who are faithful to help me break these pitfalls in my life. How about you? Are there others that you can rely on to speak honestly into your life? Do you *allow* them to speak into your life? This trap reminds me of the hamster on the round wheel racing furiously, but going nowhere.

So, here we find Naaman, the commander of an army, one who was use to making independent decisions quickly, with little input. His tendency would be to say, "I see the problem, let me fix it." (I know, I know, a typical male answer!) However, he was open to counsel and guidance. The independent nature was suppressed and he listened to those who surrounded him daily. It saved his life and opened up a new destiny for him and his family. If you find yourself identifying with the tendency to isolate and refuse the counsel of others, make the decision to open yourself up to other people. Contact several brothers or sisters and verbally commit to accountability with them. Don't wait, do it now! I'll wait to go on until you return...okay, let's continue.

It was not the counsel of his colleagues and servants that Naaman needed to wash in the Jordan. Their counsel was to listen to the higher authority, Elisha the prophet. If Elisha had said, "Jump up three times and then stand on one leg," the counsel would have been the same. Naaman chose to come under and respond to the authority that was before him. Within this decision, there was an inherent blessing. When we submit to authority, as one would submit to God, we are following a biblical principle of headship.

> *Let every soul be subject to the governing authorities. For there is no authority except from God, and the authorities that exist are appointed by God. Therefore whoever resists the authority resists the ordinance of God, and those who resist will bring judgment on themselves. For rulers are not a terror to good works, but to evil. Do you want to be unafraid of the authority? Do what is good, and you will have praise from the same.*
>
> Rom. 13:1-3

Naaman went and dipped himself in the Jordan River. The Bible says *"...and his flesh was restored like the flesh of a little child, and he was clean"* (2 Kings 5:14). What an incredible sight that must have been for the people. The miracle of cleansing must, indeed, have been a spectacular sight. But the life lesson which people carried with them was Naaman's modeling the principle of seeking something, fighting off resistance, receiving counsel and submitting to authority that ultimately brought about a miracle.

Is that the end of the story? Are these the steps to being cleansed? If all one desires is to have momentary cleansing, then yes, that is what one must do. However, if we desire to walk in a permanent victory, not falling back into a leprous situation, we must do one more thing. It is this "one more thing" I did to be sure my cleansing was complete from my recent episode. I knew I needed to come under authority in the church (spiritually—Jesus, naturally—my pastor). Then I needed to make some declarations. It was imperative that I spoke words of truth and commitment to prevent that door from remaining open.

Naaman did this very thing to ensure his healing was complete. He repented and then took a stand for righteousness by making godly declarations over his life. Naaman was cleansed, but did not want to lose his healing. How many times have you had a "breakthrough" in a spiritual area only to have it lost in the coming days due to anger, jealousy, arrogance, pride or any other number of sinful traps? This is not only frustrating, but often becomes discouraging. By taking the next step, Naaman was able to break this fleshly pattern and make a statement of permanence that prevented the enemy from stealing his cleansing.

6. *Naaman repented and took a stand toward righteousness.*
There is no certainty that seeds, when planted, will germinate into a plant. There are many factors that can interfere with the seed growing to maturity. Each year we plant a garden in our backyard. We have a large garden

spot where we plant tomatoes, squash, zucchini, spinach, raspberries, peppers, pumpkins and anything else we may get excited about that particular year. One year, we planted our garden and waited in anticipation for a beautiful harvest. However, several days after planting, it began to rain. For the next week or so, the sun was nowhere to be found as the skies poured down water. When it finally relented, our beautifully planted garden was a swamp land. Many seeds had washed away and those that didn't rotted out in a period of a few weeks. The only answer was to replant the garden.

What are we doing to prevent the seed of purification from being robbed by "the downpour of discouragement?" Are we taking steps to insure that our cleansing will take root in our spirit? If anyone has lost their healing, their cleansing because of the downpour from the clouds of life, the answer may be to replant your seeds. It does take extra time, finances and energy, but it is the only way to yield a harvest after your first planting is lost. Before we continue, take a moment and reflect on your life. If there are areas where you feel cheated, ripped off due to lost seeds, pray for God's replenishing power in your life.

> *Help us, O Lord, to replant our seeds of life. We give up the hurt and disappointment from those areas of shattered dreams and hopes. Only You can touch us and minister to us, in such a way, that life is restored and our future is bright once again. You hold the power of life and death in your hands. Release new life to us in this hour. Protect our new seeds from the winds of offense, from the birds of prey and from the lies of the enemy. Thank You, precious Father, for caring so*

> *much for us that we are allowed to step back into Your presence and Your will by simply speaking words of repentance and words of love. We love You Lord.*

God wants to restore and replenish our dreams in life. What did Naaman do to replant his seeds and prevent them from being washed away again?

It is important to remember that Naaman was not an Israelite. He did not believe in Jehovah, the God of Israel. Without the encouragement and direction from the Israeli servant girl, Naaman would never have left his land in search of Elisha. Once he received the cleansing, Naaman realized he needed to solidify the healing. This process begins as he realizes who is truly God of the earth.

> *And he returned to the man of God, he and all his aides, and came and stood before him; and he said, "Indeed, now I know that there is no God in all the earth, except in Israel...."*
>
> 2 Kings 5:15

It is here that Naaman begins to understand the true nature of God, His healing power, His sovereign plan, and His love for His children.

The next several verses find Naaman declaring that he will serve God. He declares that he will no longer sacrifice to idols, but only to God. He explains that by virtue of his job, he must enter into the pagan temples and kneel before the idols. The king used Naaman to lean on as a support, while he worshipped the false gods. We find Naaman asking the Lord for forgiveness for any improprieties in this area. While the Bible doesn't tell us what takes place when Naaman returns, I believe God found a way to spare him the indignities of bowing down before those idols. Who knows, as a new believer, Naaman may have been so evangelistic he may have brought salvation to his entire family. Regardless, Naaman chose to exalt God for the healing and verbally declared the greatness of the Lord. He chose humility and faithfulness for his life and proclaimed a pathway to righteousness. Naaman was no longer known as a leper, but instead, he was seen as a man of faith and of purity.

A Few A, B, C's (and D's & E's) to Obtaining a Cleansing

- **A**sk God to cleanse us from the defilement received from evil reports. We must examine attitudes, comments and offenses in our lives. As we go before God and present our lives, He will show us those areas of repentance that must take place. *"I beseech you therefore, brethren, by the mercies of God, that you present your bodies a living sacrifice, holy, acceptable to God, which is your reasonable service"* (Rom. 12:1). As Naaman went before **his king**, we must go before **our King**.

- **B**e diligent in prayer during this season. While there are many people who may have defiled you with their words, likewise, you may have defiled many with your words. Begin to pray for those people you have injured and inadvertently, created a stumbling block in their walk with God. Ask God to bless those who have injured you and to reveal His glory to them. The Bible tells us to *"bless those who curse you, and pray for those who spitefully use you"* (Luke 6:28).

- **C**ontinually cleanse your thoughts and your mind. Listen to worship music, keep the prayers of God on your lips, refuse to speak evil of others. We will be tempted by people and by our own thought life, but we must refrain from falling back into those habit patterns. Don't believe a report to be true because it sounds convincing. *"The simple believes every word, But the prudent considers well his steps"* (Prov. 14:15).

- **D**eliver yourself from the hands of the enemy by speaking truth about others as well as yourself. Bless those around you, pouring love upon them in speech and action. Allow the goodness of God to be an active part of your life, regardless of whether you are shopping, working, driving or sitting in your home. The light of Christ should be evident in all situations. *"Love suffers long and is kind; love does not envy; love does not parade itself, is not puffed up; does not behave rudely, does not seek its own, is not provoked, thinks no evil; does not rejoice in iniquity, but rejoices in the truth"* (1 Cor. 13:5, 6).

- **E**xamine your motives in life. Why are you saying certain things? Why are you listening to certain people? Are you willing to repent to those you have injured verbally or in your actions? God may see what we deem as appropriate or permissible, as defiling. Seek the counsel of others and pray for God's discernment in this area of your life. *"All the ways of a man are pure in his own eyes, But the Lord weighs the spirits"*(Prov. 16:2).

The cleansing process is not always enjoyable to go through, but in the end, it feels so nice. May we all be able to stand before God and know that we received His guidance and wisdom when speaking about other people. God wants us to be in unity and one in spirit. When we refuse to be a part of false stories, evil comments and innuendoes, God is able to pour a blessing upon each one of our families and on us. Encourage one another and speak in ways that edify the body of Christ. *"Behold, how good and how pleasant it is for brethren to dwell together in unity!"* (Psa. 133:1).

Questions—Examining the Heart

1. Are you able to go before God and declare yourself pure from being defiled by evil reports? If not, take time to repent and declare His cleansing.

2. Are there people you need to begin to speak blessing over instead of curses?

3. If you can think of anyone who speaks evil toward others, what steps do you need to take to avoid them or confront them?

CLOSER TO HOME

CHAPTER 12

CLOSER TO HOME
(A few final thoughts)

Kirk and Amber are a precious couple with three beautiful children. They have had a few rocky moments in their marriage, but through various times of receiving counseling, attending marriage seminars and pressing into God, they have been able to overcome many obstacles. Unfortunately, one area that they have been unable to conquer is the tendency to become offended at people. When they do, their lips begin to speak forth words of negativity toward anyone who will listen.

There was the time Amber felt other children in the church were mistreating their five-year-old daughter. She called up one of the pastors and spoke very harshly and critically toward a number of children who had called her daughter names and pushed her down. Amber then proceeded to call up a number of people and pass on her frustration. Through a series of meetings, Amber and Kirk realized there had been somewhat of a misunderstanding as their child had pushed another child first, then a retaliation occurred. While not condoning the aggression on either child's part, the complete picture did help them to see that the verbal and physical assault upon their child was not without provocation. They apologized to the pastor and continued on with life. Over the next few weeks, Kirk and Amber were openly friendly and supportive with the pastor and the general direction of the church. However, their previous contact with others had spread a seed of discontent into other families. This seed grew into a large plant in one of the families and created disunity between the husband and wife for several weeks.

About two weeks after the first incident, Kirk and Amber's oldest teenager told a high school youth leader, "My dad and mom don't think you do a good job caring about us. They say you don't watch us very closely when we are in our meetings." It was not a day or two later, that another altercation took place with their youngest daughter. This time, the daughter turned to the Sunday school teacher saying, "My parents said I don't have to come if you are going to let the kids beat me up." Both the youth leader and Sunday school teacher were at a loss as to what to say or do in the situation. The parents were undermining the authority and respect for the leaders, yet were not coming and discussing it with anyone directly.

Later that year, during the time of our annual teen camp retreat, Kirk and Amber began to see the "fruit" of their defilement. Approximately 250 teenagers, from within our network of churches were in attendance. However, Kirk and Amber's two teenagers did not want to attend. The children spoke angrily and bitterly toward the leaders and other members of the youth group. Kirk and Amber were beside themselves, asking for intervention, prayer and encouragement as their children seemed to be slipping away. They wanted their children to be a part of the camp, to attend church and grow closer to God. However, many conversations with their children were now spent arguing over whether "God was real" and whether going to church was "really that important." Throughout this time, they were oblivious to the poisonous words they had spoken in recent months and how they had impacted their family.

What conversations occur at **your** dinner table? Are the words that you share in your home supportive of authority and leadership or do you give the subtle impressions that you disagree? In your home, how do you speak about your supervisors, your friends and your spouse — all within earshot of little listening ears? Defilement is passed on from one person to another, from husband to wife, from father to son, mother to daughter and from one generation to the next. What are you passing on to your children and to those in your home? Are you a comforter or a complainer? A worshipper or a whiner? A prayer warrior or a self-centered whimperer?

I Should Know Better

It was the first day of school and our teenage son, Aaron, came home talking about his classes. Math, history, business—the usual list of classes for a junior in high school. All seemed fine until he mentioned his English class. Aaron enrolled in an advanced English class this year, whereas last year he was in a regular English class. We did not think anything of it, as Aaron receives excellent grades and enjoys school. "English is a bummer," he said. "Last year the teacher assigned a book for the students to read over the summer. Since I wasn't in her class last year, I didn't know we had to have it read by the first day of class and now I have two weeks to read this 600-paged book. Then, I have to write a report and take a test." My wife and I looked at each other, our eyes saying to one another, "The other kids had *all summer* to read their book, but our son has only two weeks?" Almost without thinking, or rather, without thinking at all, I blurted out, "Your teacher isn't being very fair. If you don't want to stay in that class Aaron, we can get your schedule changed."

Here I was, in the midst of writing about evil reports and giving myself new material for my own book. Is that what you call an autobiography? Fortunately, my son had been taught a stronger foundation. He replied, "No, I'll stay. It will just be a lot of work for the next couple of weeks." I was embarrassed by my reaction to the situation. I almost caused my son to stumble due to my own lack of discipline with my tongue. I was putting a disrespect and a doubt about his teacher's wisdom and skill into his spirit. Over the next few days, when we mentioned Aaron's schedule and the teacher's name to other parents, they all spoke highly of her, saying how much he will love her class. I have since apologized to my son and explained the danger of what I said to him. Our homes can be a breeding ground for purity or pollution.

When I worked in the public school system, it was common to find students who would hide behind their parent's anger and frustration toward the school. At times, the parental feelings were bore out of their own negative school experiences. Comments such as, "So what if my child isn't doing well in math. I didn't do well either and yet I made it" were frequently heard in one form or another. As adults, our personal perspectives carry tremendous weight in the eyes of the youth. Don't believe the lie that says the younger generation doesn't listen to older people. That is false. They listen; they watch; and they make judgments based on an adult's character and integrity in a situation. What are we modeling to those around us?

One of the most tragic examples of a parent's trying to poison their own offspring is the story of King Saul and his son, Jonathan. As discussed in earlier chapters, Saul constantly spoke polluting stories about David. He cursed David, told lies about him and did everything in his power to destroy David's reputation and his life. However, through it all, Jonathan refused to be defiled. He held fast to the biblical principle of not being a false witness, thus refusing to be used as his father's weapon by speaking bitter words. *"Who sharpen their tongue like a sword, and bend their bows to shoot their arrows—bitter words"* (Psa. 64:3). Jonathan was an exceptionally strong spiritual person. Most of us would, (and have), succumbed to this type of barrage from another person—not Jonathan, a man who made a covenant with David to be honest and true to his friend. Jonathan refused to let an evil report tarnish his perspective of the person to whom he was committed. I hope my own children will live by that example of commitment and character.

Unfortunately, not all people are able to be like Jonathan when confronted by negative comments. Many times, these words separate people, even creating divisiveness between husband and wife, parents and children, employer and employee, pastors and members. Earlier in this book, we discussed Absalom and his separation from his father, David. At the end of his life, Absalom was found saying, *"I have no son to keep my name in remembrance"* (2 Sam. 18:18). It was at this time that he built a memorial unto himself. Poor Absalom! He was all alone, no children to pass on a legacy, a vision of the future that could carry his name forward. But, is that accurate? Was Absalom without family?

Absalom was a bitter man. He was angry at his father, King David, for not seeking revenge upon Amnon for the assault on Tamar. He felt abandoned and alone. Would the offense that Absalom had impact those around him, those in his own family? In 2 Samuel 14:27, we find a very telling scripture. *"To Absalom were born three sons, and one daughter whose name was Tamar."* Indeed, Absalom had sons. And, in addition, he had a daughter that he named after his sister. Why would Absalom say later in life that he had no sons? Could it be that he created a division between his children and himself? Were they so estranged in relationship that he disowned them (or they disowned him)? While not being totally sure what occurred, it is safe to say that Absalom's defiled spirit created such dissension in his own family that he was left alone in the latter stages of his life. At all cost, we must protect our children from being polluted by evil reports and false stories. It will interfere with their destiny and future in God.

When our oldest son Jason was twelve or thirteen years old, he was just beginning his involvement in our church youth group. He seemed to enjoy it and, in fact, became close with one of the couples in leadership. He babysat their little children and went to the lake with their family. As the year progressed, we began to notice a slow, gradual change in our son. He would occasionally say a negative comment about the youth pastor or question why they had "another" youth meeting. We were surprised to hear these things as he had always enjoyed youth activities in the past. It wasn't long before Joyce and I were presented with the whole picture. These particular leaders began to openly speak against the pastors, the elders and the other children in the church. "You're expecting too much from kids," the couple stated when our senior pastor encouraged all the teenagers to sit up front in our church, instead of in the back. "Too many meetings," they proclaimed when the youth pastor called the youth to a night of prayer for the city. "We need to let kids be kids," they shouted when the youth were challenged to avoid certain movies, magazines and to be pure in their interactions with the opposite sex.

We talked with the individuals involved, but they refused to listen to another perspective—the perspective of parents whose son was being poisoned. Negative comments, twisted statements and a defiling heart were trying to infiltrate my son's life. My wife and I prayed fervently, took counsel with some friends and talked with our son. We all came to the conclusion that it was necessary to minimize contact with these people. Eventually, they left *our* church, then *another* church. A once loving marriage became full of anger and bitterness. A divorce ensued and their family was torn apart. Their children, by this couple's own admission, have struggled in negotiating the road of life. Offense and defilement ravaged a marriage and family, leaving hurt feelings and wounded lives along the way.

To this day, we use Jason's incident as an illustration of how we need to be careful as to whom and what we listen to in life. Jason has graduated from college and is living in Northern California. He has been working on his own for almost three years. However, whenever he speaks of his supervisor, colleagues or friends, he carefully watches his words. Comments of frustration are quickly balanced with words of perspective and personal ownership. It was a valuable lesson, one that could have been devastating to our own family.

Our children will test our spirits and reactions to many situations. If they are challenged in a life struggle, they may look for us to ally ourselves with them. When they are struggling with a situation, do we rescue by consoling them without pursuing God's intentions for the matter? Too often, we come to their defense at the expense of a teacher, a youth pastor, a boss or another child. I am not advocating ignoring our children or letting them suffer emotionally. But, as hard as it is to imagine, my (or your) child might be wrong. He may have embellished a situation to benefit himself. Do we rush to defend our children only to find out that later they were the ones who should be apologizing? There are practical, biblical interventions which when utilized draw a child closer to God and to the family. The following guidelines may help you to prevent deception from creeping into your home. They may also help prevent you from being the one who brings it into your home.

1. *Guard the door of your house.* If you hear people speaking false reports in your home, take authority over the situation. Boldly say, "I'd rather we not talk about someone who isn't here." If one of your children's friends is giving an evil report, interrupt them and set the boundaries. Your home should be a haven of peace and godliness. As a

parent, we must guide and direct those placed within our care. *"He who keeps instruction is in the way of life..."* (Prov. 10:17a). Model to your family that you care about their life by protecting them from the pollution and contamination of negative comments.

2. Be accountable with your own speech. In a marriage, the couple should hold each other accountable for purity in their speech. Sit down with your spouse, ask them to help you discipline your speech patterns. Honestly, even if your spouse is not a believer in Jesus Christ, they will respond to your desire for cleanliness. Speak clearly with your words. Stay away from *maybe, perhaps, but,* and be accountable for your actions. We must quit justifying our sin and accept the responsibility and consequences of our behavior. If I have spoken evil of another, there is no justification or rationale which will biblically support me. No one likes to have their character destroyed by harsh words. We must pour out to others what we would like back in return. Remember the Golden Rule? *"Therefore, whatever you want men to do to you, do also to them for this is the Law and the Prophet"* (Matt. 7:12). Let's raise up a standard of righteousness in our homes.

3. Set up ground rules with your children. Be sure to include your children in the accountability area. How do they talk about their "friends"? Would you, as an adult, allow your children to speak truth into your life and tell you to stop giving an evil report? Would you, as a son or daughter, allow your parents to challenge your speech habits in an effort to bring freedom to your life? Take one day and have each family member keep track of how many defiling comments are made about people. Have a reward at the end of the day if you are maturing in your spiritual discipline. If you find that the tongue is out of control, have a repentance "party." Play some worship music and pray for one another, drawing closer in your commitment to purity.

4. *Check for poison in the house.* Have you spoken negatively about your children's teachers? How many times have you "questioned" the minister at your church in a way that creates disunity and disharmony in the body of Christ? When your children feel challenged by the youth pastor, have you supported the challenge or undermined it? Sit down with your family and discuss attitudes toward leaders, friends and authorities in life. Ask one another how they perceive those within the family. Do the children respect the adults and vice-versa? Latent poison will eventually become active. It will not remain in its dormant state forever. And when it erupts, it will spew forth a foul spray, one that will contaminate all within its boundaries.

> *Pursue peace with all people, and holiness, without which no one will see the Lord: looking carefully lest anyone fall short of the grace of God; lest any root of bitterness springing up cause trouble, and by this many become defiled.*
>
> Heb. 12:15

5. *Examine your attitude and change it.* "*I implore Euodia and I implore Syntyche to be of the same mind in the Lord*" (Phil. 4:2). We find Paul pleading with two people, two sisters in the Lord, to stop arguing and bickering. It's not that we have to agree with people all the time. Of course we will have differences of opinion, different ways of seeing things, however, we must find a place of unity in God. I remember hearing the analogy of four people looking at a house. One was on the east side, one on the west side, yet another on the south side and a final one on the north

side. When asked to describe the house, they all had different descriptions. Independently, they were not in agreement, yet the descriptions, when put together, completed a picture of the house. Each one was correct, but no one picture was complete without the others. I was recently in a meeting with a couple frustrated with some decisions being made in the church. The senior pastor and I were listening to their perspective. At the conclusion, the pastor said, "I appreciate your viewpoint and I understand how you might see it that way, but, as the leader of this church, similar to the CEO of a company, I have a larger perspective. I must listen to the board, the people and then make a decision. I don't expect everyone to always agree with me." Then, turning to me, he continued, "I'm sure Mike, as one of my assistant pastors, doesn't agree with me all the time. However, he does support the direction and vision that we are traveling. Are you willing to support that same vision?" This encapsulated the entire issue. To speak in an aggressive, defiling manner toward another person comes against that person's vision and direction. If this happens to be a supervisor, teacher, pastor or any person in authority, it will create confusion and dissension among the people.

6. *Repent, Repent, Repent.* If you have undermined or defiled another person, you must come to the Lord with a contrite heart. *"...A broken and contrite heart—these, O God, you will not despise"* (Psa. 51:17). You may feel it necessary to go directly to the person and ask for their forgiveness. The Jewish religion has a High Holy Day called Yom Kippur that means "The Day of Atonement." On this day, each year, they gather in synagogues across the world to repent for their sins. If they have sinned against God, they ask for His forgiveness. If the sin was against another person, they seek that person out and ask for

their forgiveness. However, as Christians, each day is our "Day of Atonement." If we sin against man, we sin against God. The Bible does not encourage "repenting" in our closets. Rip off the funeral shroud of guilt and condemnation. The enemy wants us to have a pity party, but God wants us to have a repentance party. Be honest, and if necessary, atone for your defiling speech. Be cleansed by repenting and speaking cleansing words over others.

7. *Utilize the antidote for poison—LOVE.* This is the antidote we have been given by our Savior. God is love. We need to combat our anger and bitterness with love.

> *A new commandment I give to you, that you love one another; as I have loved you, that you also love one another. By this all will know that you are My disciples, if you have love for one another.*
>
> John 13:34, 35

May we all desire to be true disciples of Christ.

8. *Teach your children, your church and friends the process found in Matthew 18.* The Bible gives us a clear and concise process to follow in the event we become offended or upset. In Matthew 18:15-17, we find an outline to achieve restoration among brothers and sisters. *"Moreover if your brother sins against you, go and tell him his fault between you and him alone. If he hears you, you have gained a brother"* (v. 15). Carefully, and with gentleness, express your concerns to the person. Explain your perception and how it impacted you personally. Be open to hearing their interpretation and the possibility that you may have offended them. If the person repents and asks forgiveness, be encouraged in God for the reconciliation process. Be sure to speak forgiveness and love to the person. If the person does not repent, be careful to not fall into carnal emotions. Seek

guidance from the Holy Spirit and re-approach the person (maybe at another time). You should continue to dialogue with them until you feel God release you from this portion of the process. *"But if he will not hear, take with you one or two more, that by the mouth of two or three witnesses every word may be established"* (v. 16). This is the tricky part as the people often chosen to go with a person are biased and only serve to provoke the situation. Be sure the other person sees those going with you as godly people, walking in obedience and integrity. Again, speak in a manner of gentleness and humility, but being forthright in your concerns. If they repent, show forgiveness and blessings toward them. *"And if he refuses to hear them, tell it to the church"* (v. 17a). I have read and heard many different interpretations of "telling it the church." To me, the verse speaks of going before the leadership, the elders and the authorities in the church. I don't think, at this point, there would need to be a public meeting or a statement from the pulpit. Utilize the leadership in the church to hear the grievance and give counsel. Again, the purpose is to seek restoration and reconciliation for a problem, not to expose someone. If they repent, follow the above suggestions in making peace with your brother or sister. *"But if he refuses even to hear the church, let him be to you like a heathen and a tax collector"* (v. 17b). It is at this stage, it **may** be necessary to let the congregation know of the unwillingness of the person to repent and move away from sin. Treating them as a heathen would mean your contact with them would be focused on leading them back to God. You would speak of restoration and healing, not baseball, movies or shopping. Socializing with the person would be for the purpose of bringing him or her back into fellowship with Jesus Christ. As we look at the scriptures, Jesus connected with the heathen and tax collectors for one purpose, and one purpose only, to bring them into relationship with the Father. This may seem harsh or too rigid, but remember what fellowshipping with a defiled person can do to you. If you can't remember, return to page one and read through this text again.

By following the above eight guidelines, our homes should have a sweeter aroma and our children kept safe from the defilement of evil reports.

I recently read a story from Billy Graham regarding the area of gossip. As you read the final words of this book, allow God to consecrate your life in a way that will prevent defilement from ever creeping into your speech or listening habits. Thank you for reading this book with an open heart and mind. I trust you have found the words to be instructional and encouraging in your walk with Christ. May God richly bless each one of you in your life's endeavors.

GOSSIP
Reverend Billy Graham

There is a story of a woman in England who came to her vicar with a troubled conscience. The vicar knew her to be an habitual gossip—she maligned nearly everyone in the village.

"How can I make amends?" she pleaded. The vicar said, "If you want to make peace with your conscience, take a bag of goose feathers and drop one on the porch of each one you have slandered."

When she had done so, she came back to the vicar and said, "Is that all?" "No," said the wise old minister, "you must go now and gather up every feather and bring them all back to me."

After a long time the woman returned without a single feather. "The wind has blown them all away," she said. "My good woman," said the vicar, "so it is with gossip. Unkind words are easily dropped, but we can never take them back again."

Copyright 1976 Billy Graham Evangelistic Association, used by permission, all rights reserved.

BIBLIOGRAPHY

Anderson, Neil. *The Bondage Breaker*. Harvest House Publishers: Eugene, 1993.

Bevere, John. *The Bait of Satan*. Creation House Publications: Lake Mary, 1997.

Parrot, Les. Chapter Six, "The Gossip." *High Maintenance Relationships*. Tyndale House Publishers: Wheaton, 1996.

Sande, Ken. *The Peacemaker*. Baker Book House: Grand Rapids, 1991.

To order this book, tapes or contact the author, write to:

**Michael Sedler
Harvest Christian Fellowship
1316 North Lincoln Street
Spokane, WA. 99201
(509) 327-3278
(509) 327-6718 (Fax)
e-mail: harvest@spocom.com**

Michael Sedler is available for leadership training sessions as well as other speaking engagements such as church ministry, conferences or retreats. He has been involved in training programs throughout the Northwest and Canada. Dr. Sedler has worked extensively with schools, churches and businesses. You will find his approach to be both practical and informative.

Stairway to Deception :

50851